THE INNOVATION MATRIX

3 moves to design a winning strategy for Innovation & Intellectual Property

BY DEEPIKA JEYAKODI & MIRJAM E. ROS

BIS Publishers
Building Het Sieraad
Postjesweg 1
1057 DT Amsterdam
The Netherlands
T +31 (0)20 515 02 30
bis@bispublishers.com
www.bispublishers.com

ISBN 978-90-6369-520-0

Art Directed and Designed by Rachel Ericson-Carmiggelt | www.rachelericson.com
Edited by Femke Riemersma | femkeriemersma@gmail.com
Copyedited by Ashley Cowles | www.ashleycowles.nl
Illustrated by Simone Prick @ BuroBrand | www.burobrand.nl
Guest Authors (Legal Design Thinking) Stefania Passera | www.stefaniapassera.com & Helena Haapio | www.lexpert.com

The book *The Innovation Matrix* expresses the writers' personal views. The content does not reflect the ideas of any of the
entities with which Mirjam and Deepika are or have been affiliated.

For all the innovators working towards
making this world a better place for everyone.

—*Deepika Jeyakodi & Mirjam E. Ros*

table of contents

E = Example

move 1
THINK
INTERNAL & EXTERNAL ANALYSIS

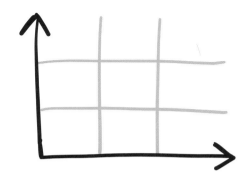

move 2

STRATEGIZE

GATHERING YOUR INNOVATION & IP OPTIONS

move 3
ACT
STRATEGY IMPLEMENTATION

go!
PLAY
3 CASES THAT PULL IT ALL TOGETHER

preface

One random day in 2016, we were discussing a presentation that Mirjam had given at a conference in Rome, on open innovation and intellectual property (IP). She had received exceptional feedback about her session, yet she seemed surprised. Mirjam asked me, 'But, isn't this so simple and logical?' It was logical, yes, but not that simple.

What started out as a simple discussion between two people who shared common interests in the subject gradually evolved into a paper and then a book. In the two years since we started writing this book, the many people we have crossed paths with and our interactions with them have inspired us and expanded our knowledge further. Working together helped us recognize our strengths and weaknesses as individuals, which in turn enabled us to complement each other and grow stronger together. What a ride!

At each step of writing The Innovation Matrix, we hoped to simplify and structure innovation and IP management and strategy, to facilitate your innovation team as a whole! We truly believe that a team can sprint towards success only when 'everyone has their noses in the same direction', as the Dutch would say.

In today's world, a master 'specialist' is a great asset to the team, but such a master also needs to zoom out and maintain a helicopter view on what the team does and needs, in order to work together cohesively. Innovation teams need to be interdisciplinary in terms of team composition, and multidisciplinary in their approach to the problems they seek to address.

Work and knowledge should not be compartmentalized. Contracts and legal people will do well to learn from business people, engineers, innovators, and vice versa. We have tried to stress these aspects in the different chapters of our book, hoping that our work will inspire you to look at innovation and IP from a new perspective.

Mirjam's note

At university, while studying Public Administration and Policy, a key take-away was to be multidisciplinary. I learned to look at things from different angles, including those of others. I learned that one could never fly alone!

My interest to work with multidisciplinary teams led to my career choice working with Commercial, Contracts and Legal, Business Strategy and Organizational Development. I recognized that in order to achieve success in business and innovation, different disciplines had to come together.

In the early 2000s, to further hone my skills, I decided to pursue a specialization in Business Law. The course encompassed elements of law, commercial contracts, and IP. It was very different from what I actually did in the office. At work, we co-operated more and more with external partners in innovation teams and with that, the urgency for robust IP agreements became greater. While at university, I learnt about legislation outlining principles on protecting IP. Most companies were applying standard terms and conditions to innovation agreements in which they claimed the IP in accordance with the law, creating tension between partners, suppliers, and customers. Criteria for a more fair and simple distribution of IP with business sense were missing. Lots of new open innovation experiments and innovative IP set-ups arose, but how they distributed IP and to what extent this supported and speeded up the innovation process was not shared and used openly, nor broadly. This meant a gap between theory and practice.

It seemed counterproductive and it got me thinking about improvements that might add more fairness, efficiency, and speed to negotiations and innovations. Thus began my innovation and IP Journey. In my thesis, I proposed criteria that can help analyze innovation in any commercial context, and how IP can be distributed between project parties based on the outcomes of the analysis. Ten years later, I met my co-author, Deepika...

Deepika's note

Having studied in fourteen schools, I had to learn to make friends fast, be open to new things, pick up diverse interests, and retain some of them before I moved again. Years later, I found I was interested in things that involved variety, be it academics or work. This book is meant to reflect some of this variety, too.

My first encounter with IP was in high school, when some of my musician/writer friends had to deal with copyright contracts. It seemed a fascinating subject. In university, I still enjoyed learning about IP law, which led to me attaining a diploma in the subject.

When I met Mirjam in 2016, I was fascinated by her efforts in trying to bridge a gap between theory and practice. I remember Mirjam laughing shyly when I urged her to write a book. At some point, she figured out that I was serious and assured me she would consider the option, if I would be her co-author. Yes! We started contemplating how to simplify the subject to make it accessible to anyone in an innovation team. We wrote, re-wrote, brainstormed, had reviews with friends and family, and wrote some more until we reached the point where we thought our work was 'not perfect, but good enough' to be shared with the world.

Our aim is to enable innovation teams as a whole to think strategically in terms of innovation and IP. In the future, we hope to collaborate with innovation teams to build a repository of worldwide best practices in innovation and IP distribution. Our intention was to narrow the gaps between theory and practice, and between academia and business. We hope this book will be a small step towards building that bridge.

Creating ideas jointly is relatively simple, but capturing their value individually is often very complicated. You need a solid strategy to hold onto. In three steps, we will enable you to construct an innovation strategy from an intellectual property (IP) perspective. This will help you successfully manage innovation in a complex and competitive business world.

THINK – STRATEGIZE – ACT

The core of this book is divided into three crucial moves: think, strategize, and act. These moves will enable you to construct your strategy on both innovation and IP, but they are also useful for decisions on partner selection, creating ideas jointly, building your business model, or discussing IP. Depending on your time, knowledge, and background, you can leap straight into move 1 (think) or first immerse yourself in the basics (introduction) to kickstart your thinking.

To make the book as hands-on as possible, we added plenty of examples, tips, checklists, and business cases based on the inno-vation landscape as we know it. Throughout the book, we have also added lines of thinking in blue to help you put the model into practice. We call these 'bringing IP into play'. The contents of this book do not constitute legal advice. For specific use, please check the local IP laws and practices too.

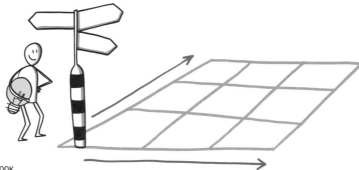

START HERE

This map will help you navigate our book the way that best suits you.
Feel free to jump straight into the framework, or start at the very beginning.

INTRODUCTION
Innovation in its changing habitat, the need for open innovation, and the use of IP as a tool.

UNDERSTANDING INNOVATION & IP
Why IP is key to managing innovation. **PAGE 14**

YOU NEED A STRATEGY
How to fit IP into your innovation strategy. **PAGE 20**

OR START HERE

FRAMEWORK MOVES 1-2-3

IDEALLY, THIS STRATEGY SHOULD COVER THESE THREE MOVES, ALTHOUGH THE PROCESS CAN BE ITERATIVE.

move 1

THINK
We have identified 6 business-savvy Building Blocks to help you analyze your business and ecosystem methodically.
PAGE 28

move 2

STRATEGIZE
In the innovation and IP Matrix, you will find 9 strategies that enable you to capture the value of your innovation in the best possible way.
PAGE 56

move 3

ACT
You now have a draft game plan for your innovation case. These 3 upcycled Tools will help you implement your strategy.
PAGE 82

PLAY
We have created 3 cases to which you can apply our framework. Also included are some considerations to guide you through the exercise.
PAGE 110

WAIT!
Have you considered these meta influencers in the present-day world?
PAGE 47

THE PLATFORM BUSINESS MODEL
The new way to do business and innovation.
PAGE 74

LEGAL DESIGN THINKING
Learn to design processes and contracts that support your team.
PAGE 93

TEMPLATES
Use these templates to focus your thoughts.

THESE TEMPLATES ARE USEFUL IN DIFFERENT STAGES OF THE CONTRACTING PROCESS

PAGE 106
Needs & contributions matrix

PAGE 107
Wedding Cake model brainstorm

PAGE 108
Building Block analysis

PAGE 109
Innovation & IP strategy term sheet

INTRODUCTION

Understanding innovation

WHY INTELLECTUAL PROPERTY IS KEY

to managing innovation

This chapter explores innovation in its changing habitat, the increasing tendency to innovating openly, and the possibility to use intellectual property (IP) not just as an asset, but as a tool. It focuses on the importance of having an innovation strategy that includes components of IP.

The War of Currents between George Westinghouse (Nikola Tesla's employer) and Thomas Alva Edison in the late 1800s was a series of events that can inspire innovators today on how to capture the value of their innovation. Westinghouse was an 'open' innovator in his day who capitalized on smart business strategies to bring life to his inventions or just support genius innovators. It seems like he was always 'looking outside' for inspiration, to the new inventions of his time, which could be combined and applied for his business and public use. One of his best strategies was to not only acquire some of Nikola Tesla's patents but to employ him, paving the way for a successful joint collaboration. Westinghouse's innovation strategy gave him a definitive edge over Edison, a defensive multi-patent holder, regarding the electrification of America. A great innovation alone cannot be a winner. To capture the value and reap the benefits of a great innovation, you need to employ the right strategy. With a great strategy, even a simple innovation can shine.

THE EVOLUTION OF INNOVATION

IP is at the core of all innovation. Back in 500 BCE, the government of the Greek state of Sybaris offered one year's patent 'to all who should discover any new refinement in luxury[1].' Since then, IP laws evolved as a way to grant an exclusive right or even a monopoly to the owner of an idea. Innovation would occur behind closed doors, ideas would be generated by chosen experts, and any knowledge or technique thus generated would be closely guarded.

Definition

INNOVATION

The sum of all steps and processes involved in turning an idea or a concept into a product, service, or experience, which is of value from a business or customer perspective.

FACTORS ENCOURAGING OPEN INNOVATION

Over the past decade, innovating openly became more and more important for organizations to survive in the modern world and stay ahead of the competition. Many organizations are convinced they can innovate faster and more efficiently when 'forces combine' because of the following developments:

Talent

Not all the talent and knowledge your organization needs is present within the organization itself. There are smarter people with better ideas out there.

Mobility

Babyboomers stay put in one organization for over 20 years, whereas Gen Y and Gen Z are mobile. People and knowledge move in and out of the organization, more frequently than they used to.

Money

It is not too hard to find funding for a good idea. The rise of venture capitalists, angel investors, crowd funders etc., shows that money is moving to where the idea or knowledge is.

Speed

The 'time to market' for many products and services has become much shorter than in the past. Therefore, there is an urgency to innovate faster. An exchange of ideas and developments can speed up innovation and shorten the time to market.

INNOVATION TODAY

In this era of competition, the lone genius has become a rarity. Anyone owning a smartphone today would know that the phone in their palm is a product of several ideas, several brains, and more importantly: the IP from several different organizations.

The complex inter-relationship between an organization and its larger environment plays an important role in shaping innovation and its success. Organizations choose to work closely with some organizations, and defensively with some others. Technological advancements and wide-spread access to information reinforce the need to be able to build and implement collaborative 'outside' strategies for innovation.

To stay successful, implementing innovation the right way within your organization and establishing the right connections with the right organizations and third parties is crucial in the current markets. It is not just the specialists who have access to business knowledge and information. The ecosystem in which the business thrives has many players, big and small—customers, suppliers, partners, R&D institutes, etc.—playing different roles that can contribute to innovation.

A VUCA WORLD

The business world today is Volatile, Uncertain, Complex and Ambiguous, or as the military would say, 'VUCA'. At the turn of each year, major political and socio-economic changes, impact global organizations. To respond to such changes, organizations need effective strategies.

The innovation landscape is gradually shifting towards knowledge pools, where businesses, as Valdis Krebs states, 'connect on similarities and benefit from their differences'.[2] Where and how to start with innovation in this more open, interconnected, and ecosystem environment? That is a fair question, because the innovation process itself is neither plain nor easy.

"I HAVE NOT FAILED, I'VE JUST FOUND 10,000 WAYS THAT WON'T WORK."

—Thomas Edison

THE ROAD TO SUCCESS: FAILING FAST TO SUCCEED

In this intricate, competitive, hyper-connected and uncertain world of business, as an organization and a person: you can't afford to wait until you know it all, whether business-related or personal. You are more likely to succeed when you learn by trial and fail fast as this allows you to be more creative and adaptive. Unfortunately, there is no one-stop solution or a one-size-fits-all approach, but a sound strategy can help navigate towards success.

OPEN INNOVATION

Henry Chesbrough propagated the concept of Open Innovation, something that has been around for ages, but had found new applicability and increased importance. He described that 'Open Innovation is how a company can use its business model to identify a more enlightened role for Research & Development (R&D) in a world of abundant information, better manage and access IP, advance its current business, and grow its future business'.[3] In plain terms, it is the process of tapping in to ideas and resources outside your business or organization, not just to advance your own innovation but to benefit the partner business or organization in some way. There are different degrees of openness in innovation, as we will later see in some examples.

In a closed setting, organizations create ideas and innovate on their own. They often protect their knowledge and rights by keeping them secret, protecting them and/or vesting IP rights on them, such as patents, copyrights, or models. In such a closed set-up, excluding others is key, and such an approach is primarily defensive. The degree of openness in working together or complementarily determines whether the innovation occurs in a closed or more open setting. This degree of openness also influences the way companies handle knowledge management and treat IP.

IP AS A TOOL FOR OPEN INNOVATION

A more open innovation model assumes a great pool of useful ideas outside the walls of the company. In this case, IP is not only used to protect ideas in order to generate revenues: the company collaborates to develop ideas, innovating together. When an organization applies this more open model—protecting IP as well as selling, sharing, or buying it—the IP portfolio will not only be used as an asset, but also as a strategic tool. As a result, the company profits when other parties use their IP and the other way around. This way, IP can be used proactively rather than just defensively.

Definition

INTELLECTUAL PROPERTY

Any product of the human intellect, recognized to be protectable by law.

Examples

→ **Physical products and processes using them**

→ **Written or recorded material**

→ **Special product design**

→ **Hardware, software, website or architectural materials**

→ **Proprietary information that gives advantage over your competitors**

→ **Unique name**

→ **People with expertise**

→ **Unique/heritage industrial knowledge**

WAYS TO USE IP AS A TOOL

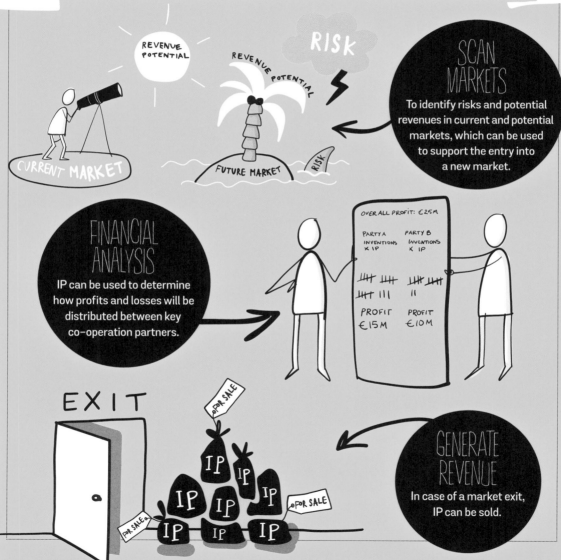

REVENUE POTENTIAL

REVENUE POTENTIAL

RISK

CURRENT MARKET

FUTURE MARKET

RISK

SCAN MARKETS
To identify risks and potential revenues in current and potential markets, which can be used to support the entry into a new market.

FINANCIAL ANALYSIS
IP can be used to determine how profits and losses will be distributed between key co-operation partners.

OVERALL PROFIT: €25M

PARTY A INVENTIONS X IP

PARTY B INVENTIONS X IP

PROFIT €15M

PROFIT €10M

EXIT

FOR SALE

IP

GENERATE REVENUE
In case of a market exit, IP can be sold.

SOURCE OF THE TEXT IN THE VISUAL: H.W. CHESBROUGH [4]

GAME ON *You need a strategy*

Organizations that want to innovate need to make sure they adopt—and adapt to—innovation the right way. Innovation is dynamic in nature; it is not a new project or department. In addition, a strategy for innovation cannot be effective unless it includes a strategy for IP. Without an IP strategy, capturing value from innovation can become difficult and even frustrating.

Not all organizations have a dedicated innovation strategy. This causes innovation to be scattered, set up by trial and error, imitating others' innovation models without analyzing one's own requirements. Not surprisingly, this does not automatically lead to success. Organizations need to look at innovation from a more strategic perspective; what are they good at, what is their current and future context, what is necessary, and how can they reach their long term goals?

Definition

STRATEGY

The total of all steps and processes that will help achieve a goal or ambition. These can be business, commercial, legal, and/or technical strategies.

"WHAT DO YOU WANT TO ACHIEVE OR AVOID? THE ANSWERS TO THIS QUESTION ARE OBJECTIVES. HOW WILL YOU GO ABOUT ACHIEVING YOUR DESIRED RESULTS? THE ANSWER TO THIS YOU CAN CALL STRATEGY."

—William E. Rothschild

VUCA 2.0

Many business gurus believe that organizations can prepare themselves to handle the VUCA world. We aim to prepare you for VUCA 2.0[5], urging you to have the Vision, Understanding, Courage, and Adaptability to succeed in your innovation endeavours.

The biggest struggle for organizations is knowing where to start and how to look at innovation from this strategic perspective. Some of the top companies worldwide have IP at the core of their strategy, be it Coca-Cola with their secret recipe or Facebook with their Open Source software. However, some organizations do not pay close attention to the strategic importance of appropriately capturing and monetizing their bright ideas, and any IP involved at the various stages of innovation. This is a major hurdle to the innovation process. Just as an example, IP plays a crucial role in facilitating access to business angels and providers of early-stage capital including seed capital, venture capitalists, financial institutions, which may provide the 'lifeline' an invention needs in order to reach the marketplace and avoid the 'valley of death'[6].

SET-UP FOR SUCCESS

Organizations usually have a set-up for innovation: procedures to identify a problem that requires a solution, to build a business plan to develop the solution, and to ascertain how resources will be organized in order to arrive at the solution. Based on this procedure, there will be a system to review the process, make decisions, so on and so forth. This system needs a strategy to function efficiently. Without a strategy, this set-up would just be chaotic. Without being able to zoom in and out on your objectives and how you get there, the task and process of innovation can end up being a very frustrating one.

STRATEGIC INNOVATION & IP CONSIDERATIONS

The laws only lay down rules for protecting, safeguarding, and using IP. Surprisingly, not so much has been written or published to answer strategic questions surrounding the innovation process and IP, such as:

- How do we deal with knowledge within an organization?

- How do we make best use of it?

- How do we select the right partner to work with?

- How do we manage knowledge exchange when working together?

- Do we protect it defensively, or do we reveal it to others?

- How do we capture value from a collaboration?

- How do we distribute IP between parties?

- How do we deal with the changing nature of an innovation process?

building your
INNOVATION & IP STRATEGY

Harnessing innovation requires firstly that it is identified as an imperative, and communicated throughout an organization. The next step would be to devise an innovation and IP strategy on how to approach innovation both within and outside the organization. **Ideally, this strategy should cover these three moves, although the process can be iterative.**

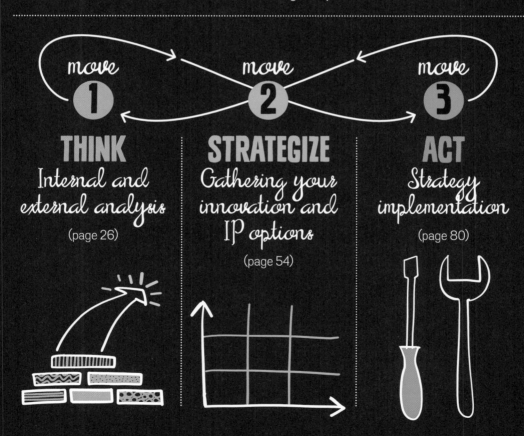

move
①
THINK
Internal and external analysis
(page 26)

move
②
STRATEGIZE
Gathering your innovation and IP options
(page 54)

move
③
ACT
Strategy implementation
(page 80)

Any innovation setting requires strong protection mechanisms, focused sharing and distribution, and effective resource management if they are to have successful and mutually beneficial relationships within and between innovation teams.

Some organizations take a one–size–fits–all approach to handling IP. Consequently, the same approach is applied to all projects, partners, and agreements. This hampers establishing a nurturing environment for innovation and also damages the relationship with your innovation partner or partners.

Creating and maintaining a strong IP strategy that allows IP management to be customized depending on various criteria, can add immense value and utility to the result or product of open innovation. Incorporating that IP strategy into the overall innovation strategy will greatly ease the management of commercial and innovation behaviour in an organization.

STRATEGY GROUNDWORK: THINGS TO DO

Organizations need to take the following internal steps in order to formulate an IP strategy for open innovation:

1. Introspect

→Identify, characterize, and classify organizational IP for innovation projects and partnerships.

→Detect restrictions, risks and business potentials on IP asset/tool use.

→Collaborate with the technical team, sales and marketing, business development, procurement and legal teams to develop an IP exploitation and management framework.

→Effectively communicate the IP framework internally and to potential alliance partners, in order to foster mutual benefits.

→Align the IP framework with the appropriate existing and future business models.

2. Realize

Organizations need to realize that successful innovation in today's world depends on a non-traditional and flexible IP approach. Firms often need to collaborate with a large number of actors from outside their organization to be able to innovate. At the same time, they need to be focused on capturing the returns from their innovative ideas. Rigid IP policies and their terms and conditions can become stumbling blocks on the way to innovation. In today's highly competitive and innovative world, your organization's commercial and management reputation should not be threatened by the blanket application of standard protective terms and conditions.

3. Adapt

Partners, suppliers, customers, and users need to identify your organization as an innovative, commercially proactive party that can make the most of such innovation and knowledge. Customizing to match the counter parties' IP utility or interest can increase aspects like co-operation, knowledge, turnover, profit, reputation, and market visibility. The only way to achieve this is by being flexible about IP negotiation both within the innovation setting and in its distribution. Such innovation-ready commercial behaviour must be accompanied by an appropriate legal response, in the form of creative and clever contracting.

INTRODUCTION
summary

1. Open innovation is the process of tapping into ideas and resources outside your business or organization, not just to advance your own innovation, but to benefit the partner business or organization in some way.

2. IP should not just be protected as an asset. It must be used as a tool for innovation. You can trade, share, and distribute it.

3. The laws only lay down rules for protecting, safeguarding, and using IP. Surprisingly, not much has been written or published to answer strategic questions surrounding innovation and how to distribute IP within the innovation partners.

4. Organizations need to be flexible about IP negotiation and its distribution within the innovation setting. A one-size-fits-all approach to handling IP hampers the establishment of a nurturing environment for innovation and damages the relationship with your innovation partner or partners.

5. An innovation and IP strategy consists of an internal and external analysis **(MOVE 1: THINK)**, innovation and IP options **(MOVE 2: STRATEGIZE)**, and strategy implementation **(MOVE 3: ACT)**.

NEXT UP THINK

move

1

THINK

Internal and external analysis

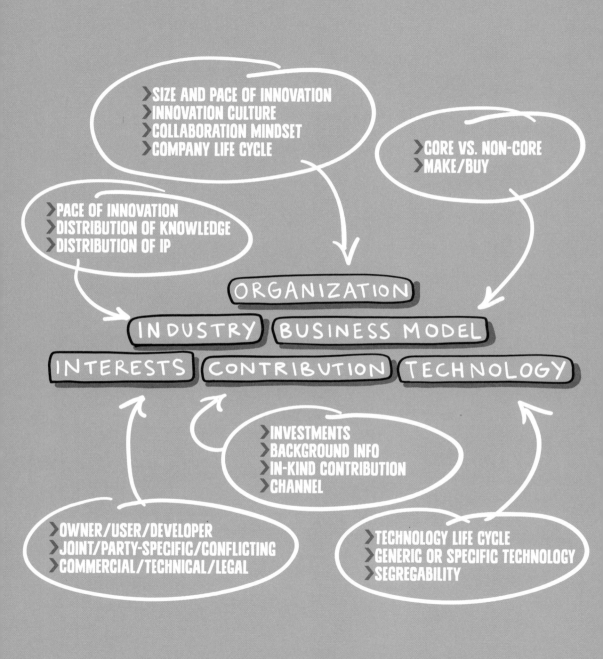

6 Building Blocks to analyze your innovation game

We have identified six Building Blocks to help you judge your organization's status, strengths, and needs regarding its innovation ambitions. Analyzing these Building Blocks will enable you to create your innovation and IP strategy.

You have a dream, a vision, or a goal for your organization. Now what? The first step after you have clearly defined your innovation goals is to perform a thorough internal and external analysis. We have identified six Building Blocks that will help you better understand your own business practice, your technology/product/service, innovation setting, IP management, your relationship with other players within the ecosystem, and your clever contracting needs. Analyzing these Building Blocks will enable you to lay the foundation for your innovation and IP strategy.

Block ① INTERESTS

Any organization successful at innovation can tell you there is an art to balancing the interests of the multiple parties involved. Examining the interests of these different parties is the most important Building Block. We identify three different kinds of interests, each of which can be a different layer in the analysis.

1. PERSPECTIVE OF THE OWNER, DEVELOPER OR USER

Interests differ depending on perspective. Are you the IP developer, owner or user?[1]. It is important to realize which perspective you take and to what extent it differs from the others, and why.

The IP owner may inherently want to be protective while a developer/enhancer may seek more access, and a user would want unhindered rights to use it. Balancing two or more of these perspectives will impact how the rest of the world sees your technology, product or service. For example, if you make your software Open Source and tell developers that any changes they make should also be Open Source, you determine how the whole effort benefits the user.

2. JOINT, PARTY-SPECIFIC OR CONFLICTING INTERESTS[2]

After reflecting on the impact your perspective as the IP owner, developer or user has, it is important to identify whether the parties involved in an innovation share the same interests or not. If the parties don't share the same interests, there are two other options: they have party-specific interests, or conflicting interests. The nature of these interests between parties influences what strategies are available. For example, when parties have a joint interest, they often share the IP with or reveal it to other parties in the ecosystem.

Tip

Identifying the interests of two or three parties is easier than doing the same for five parties or more. The more parties involved, the more complex and varied the direction can be. Even then, mapping the interests of each party may lead to an overall win-win situation.

Bringing IP into play

→ In case of shared interests, parties can consider to co-own IP with or without letting each other know, what is done with the IP. Co-owned IP does not necessarily mean the parties have exactly the same rights and obligations; this can be different. Another option is to give each other free access to the IP, or establish similar user rights. However, you must be aware of the difference between parties and of what this can mean in terms of competition. Do you want to boost the whole ecosystem, and is your pie (your accessible market) too big to eat on your own? In that case, shared IP could be a valid option. Shared IP could also be beneficial if parties are complementary with regard to work scope or if they work in different parts of the value chain, since they will probably not compete with each other in the same market.

→ In case of party-specific interests, it is relatively simple; the results of the innovation and the value captured from it, including but not limited to IP, can be easily distributed amongst the parties.

In this case, you could use the Wedding Cake model to distribute the IP between parties, so each partner gets the piece of cake they want. You may choose to keep the whole cake yourself (sole ownership), share it equally with another (co-ownership), or distribute slices of the cake to partners and maybe even third parties. (For more information on the Wedding Cake model, see Move 2 page 67).

→ If parties have conflicting innovation interests, it is important to choose a model that will be able to neutralize this. You can use the Wedding Cake model to carefully split IP between parties and register it separately, or license specific interests therein. A situation of co-ownership is usually not ideal when there are conflicting interests at play. Sometimes, it is better to consider innovating with another party.

Block ❶ INTERESTS

3. TECHNICAL, COMMERCIAL AND LEGAL INTERESTS

These interests pertain to the more objective part of innovation. Interests can be broadly distinguished into technical, commercial, and legal interests. The innovation process starts with the technical potential of that innovation. The question is whether its technical potential can be turned into real–life commercial value, which can be captured via a solid business model. Capturing value in the commercial sense is possible when there are adequate legal arrangements in place that give you certain protection by rights and responsibilities or if, by revealing the innovation, the business gets a boost.

This is not an either–or scenario; each organization will emphasize and act based on its unique combination of interests. For example, in the USA (leading innovation worldwide), most innovations have been publicly funded. Strong bonds between academia and industry increase the chances for innovation. Clearly, these two sides do not have the same objective interests. While academia will place more importance on the technical and scientific side, business will prioritize commercial and legal interests.

Despite the differences, a strategic combination of interests that best suits each organization is picked whenever facing a choice regarding a particular case. It is never only the technology, money, or legal protection that turns an innovation into a success.

Tip

By listing the different interests of the parties involved, you will better understand the reasoning and positions of these parties. Consequently, you will be able to maneuver negotiations in a better manner. Often, good insight into the different types of interests will lead to more creative solutions.

→When different organizations collaborate and consolidate IP within an ecosystem and go on to capture value together, they must be careful not to violate competition law. One way to avoid such circumstances is by arranging the exclusivity or non–exclusivity in terms of the different parties' interests, keeping in mind the rules at play on a national and international level.

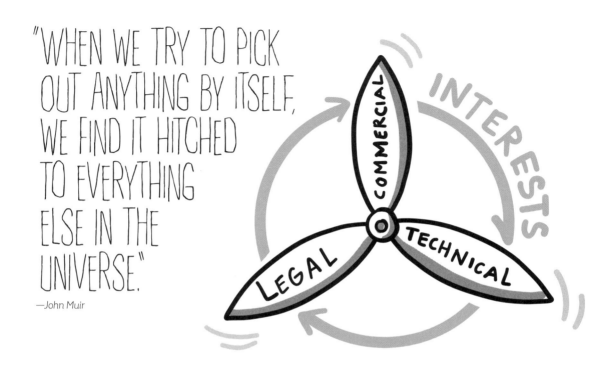

"WHEN WE TRY TO PICK OUT ANYTHING BY ITSELF, WE FIND IT HITCHED TO EVERYTHING ELSE IN THE UNIVERSE."

—John Muir

Bringing IP into play

→ **Commercial interests** could be a reason to own IP, as is creating a barrier for others to enter a market, getting access to new markets, receiving licence fees, getting access to IP from others (for example by cross-licensing), or a fair distribution of risk and reward between partners. Some organizations even choose to open up aging IP to reduce the administrative costs in maintaining the IP.

→ **Technical interests** are often linked to getting access to new research and technologies, finding complementary activities or partners to innovate, and gaining insight into research agendas and progress made by universities and technology institutes.

→ **Legal interests** such as avoiding infringement—and, consequently, litigation—can provide reasons to own or license IP. This way, you create a safe haven to shield the organization's IP on products and services.

"JOINT INNOVATION,
COST SHARING
OR DREAM SHARING?"
–Patrick de Jager

Block ② CONTRIBUTION

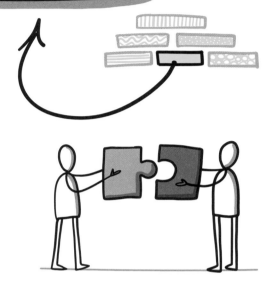

In order to determine the value of an innovation project, or estimate the return on investment, etc., first consider what the parties involved each brought in at the start of the project and will bring in during the collaboration. This can serve as a starting point to negotiate on what each party gets out of the collaboration in the end.

Tip

Contributions to look at are, for example: investments made in the past on the same effort and how much of it is brought into the present work, the value of IP or know-how brought in, or other inputs like in-kind contributions, expertise, hours of R&D work, etc. Access to markets, distribution channels, and networks are also indispensable input to an organization.

Bringing IP into play

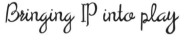

→IP law discusses joint-ownership, but says nothing about how to distribute IP and capture its value. Paying for an innovation does not automatically mean you can own the innovation's results and outcomes. Your contribution and how much that adds value to the innovation itself will greatly influence how you negotiate the IP distribution of the results and outcomes of the innovation with your partners. In case yours is the largest—or even the only—contribution to the innovation, it may be logical for you to own the results or outcomes of that innovation. If you bring in a network or channels to the market, even though you play no role in the actual development or innovation, you could still ask for user rights to capitalize on your channels or to earn a fee from any party who makes use of your channel.

EXAMPLE
FACEBOOK PARTNERS WITH PAYPAL

In late 2016, Facebook and PayPal announced a partnership wherein Facebook Messenger users can link to their PayPal accounts, to manage transactions without leaving the site[4]. While Facebook was adding a solution for its customers, it was also opening up PayPal to its 2 billion users. On the other hand, Facebook did not have to spend its resources on developing a new payment system.

Block ❸ TECHNOLOGY

What is innovation without the technology it employs, or the developments it can lead to? In order to determine what kind of technology you are or will be dealing with in the innovation process, you will need to assess the following dynamics: the technology life cycle, generic or specific technologies, and segregability.

1. TECHNOLOGY LIFE CYCLE

Often, parties collaborate at the beginning stages of the technology life cycle. When the technology matures at some point, they will split and take the result to a market. Some others will collaborate at the more mature stage to add more value to their existing product or service, or just to sustain their business. Some clever ones also find a way to collaborate when the technology has lost its value or utility either to generate new value or utility, or just to spur more innovation and/or licence revenues.

Bringing IP into play

➜ When you're in the early stage of a technology or a product's life cycle in innovation, the IP will be less mature. In other words, it will have a lower Technology Readiness Level (TRL), and is easier to share with partners. Anything can come out of it in the next stages; it may be that each partner identifies a commercial application. In case your product or technology-specific IP is at a mature stage, i.e. where you're closer to the market, it is often better to either maintain the IP yourself or make sure it is well-arranged and distributed between partners, to avoid confusion when you actually want to capture the value or monetize the innovation.

Tip
The points of entry and exit in a collaboration need to be planned carefully, depending on time and maturity of the technology, in order to derive the best value for both that technology and your organization.

Technology life cycle models

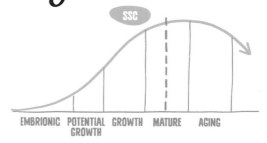

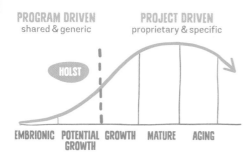

PROGRAM DRIVEN
shared & generic

PROJECT DRIVEN
proprietary & specific

EMBRIONIC POTENTIAL GROWTH MATURE AGING
          GROWTH

EMBRIONIC POTENTIAL GROWTH MATURE AGING
          GROWTH

EXAMPLE

EARLY COLLABORATION

The Holst Centre[5] is an independent R&D centre that develops technologies for wireless autonomous sensor technologies and flexible electronics in an open innovation setting and in dedicated research trajectories. Participants at this centre pay an entrance fee, which provides non-exclusive access to IP that other parties bring in.

At Holst Centre, parties collaborate in the same value chain and in the first phases of the technology life cycle. When the generic technology is applied to a prototype model, parties split up and develop it from this generic state into a more specific technology. Parties don't differentiate between innovators' products until these later stages of the technology life cycle. Here too, the main reasons for joint and open innovation are cost sharing and increasing the innovation speed.

EXAMPLE

LATE SPLIT UP

The Structural Genomics Consortium[6], (SGC) is a public-private, open access, not-for-profit organization created in 2004. Here, parties engaged in innovation work via a special model where 'firstly, all outputs produced by the SGC are made publicly available and IP restriction on use is ruled out until later stages of clinical trials. For a fixed annual sum, all SGC funders have the opportunity to determine the direction of SGC research, nominate someone to join the SGC board of directors and place scientists to work in SGC laboratories'.

The model represents a long-term, international, multiple-funder initiative with the potential to provide stability to the sector[7]. The late split up in the life cycle model is one of their core strategies: when the invention is quite mature, the parties go their own ways to develop it further and take it to market. You may wonder why the critical pharma industry engages in joint collaborations. The primary reason is that it is cheaper to collaborate, and the risk associated with innovation is much lower.

The patent arsenal is substituted with other creative means of IP distribution, thereby absorbing far more value from innovation than when defending patents developed in a closed set-up. For example, Bayer or Pfizer, partners in the SGC, would use trademarks and service to distinguish their products from the rest; rather than worry about segregability, they just use a creative method to claim each one's value.

TECHNOLOGY

EXAMPLE

VANTABLACK AND THE FIELD OF ART

When Surrey Nanosystems in the United Kingdom developed the darkest material 'Vantablack[8]' using carbon nanotubes, little did it know about its unusual use. Renowned Artist Anish Kapoor received an exclusive licence to use the coating in the field of art, prohibiting any other artist from using the darkest material available. This is a specific use for the technology, although the purpose for which it was invented was not primarily for art. On the other hand, the technology still has several generic uses.

Unlike specific technology, there are plenty of application and market options for generic technology, which determines whether or not to take a more defensive approach to the result of the innovation.

2. GENERIC OR SPECIFIC TECHNOLOGY

Is the input for, or result of innovation generic or specific in nature? What utility will you require? Unlike specific technology, generic technology is tradable widely, perhaps across different industries and their respective markets.

3. SEGREGABILITY

In some industries, such as pharma, the product of innovation is often fluid and therefore difficult to segregate, whereas in other industries, such as ICT, it may be relatively easier to identify who contributed to what portion of the technology. This requires careful consideration, particularly when the development takes places in a public–private set-up. Certain national laws do not allow exclusive rights for commercialization by one party if public funds have been used in the innovation process. Other national laws may also require parties to publish or to provide open access to their innovation or development research.

Bringing IP into play

→ If IP is segregable, it is easier to distribute between the innovating parties. If it is non-segregable, you will most probably co-own the IP. Even so, you can choose to distribute the user rights creatively based on other Building Blocks, like using the Wedding Cake model to determine IP distribution.

"IT'S NOT JUST THE TECHNOLOGY,
IT'S THE BUSINESS MODEL!"

—Cathy Lasser

Block 4 BUSINESS MODEL

BUSINESS MODEL: CORE AND NON-CORE

As Cathy Lasser from IBM says: "It's not the technology, it's the business model!" A business model has two purposes: creating value and capturing value[9]. Creating value is about developing a new product or service that has potential value. The next step is to use a business model that translates the technical potential into a net commercial value for the company. The technology itself has no objective value; its worth is undefined until it is commercialized. The value of the innovation increases when the innovation is—or is close to—your core business, and can be launched in a strategic application or market. It is therefore important to assess whether the innovation is core or non-core business. The innovation has no value if you do not apply the most apt business model: average technology sold via a fantastic business model will always generate more value than great technology commercialized through an average business model.

Tip

You may wonder why we use the term 'business model' for the technology and not for your organization. We believe the result or product of each innovation exercise deserves its own business model. Doing this is the only way you will be able to factor in the flexibility of working in the ecosystem or even distributing IP.

HIGH VALUE INNOVATION

FOCUS ON YOUR core

STRATEGIC TECHNOLOGY

STRATEGIC MARKET

NON CORE	CORE!
NON CORE	NON CORE

Bringing IP into play

→For negotiators, contracts and legal professionals, knowing what is core and non-core is key. That way, they can spend time on what is important for the innovation. Too often, time and money is wasted on discussions on non-core IP and its business model.

→Freedom to operate or user rights pertaining to IP are essential to fully use your business model. Especially if you use another organization's IP—perhaps a supplier from whom you buy something off-the shelf to incorporate into your product or technology—it is important to clearly establish guarantees on the use of their IP and on managing possible infringement. When using a third party's IP in your core, it would be wise to arrange indemnifications or exclusions. The last thing you want is to engage in a litigation where someone else is suing the third-party for infringement.

→For non-core IP, licensing in or out could be an option. Such IP can also be given away for free, or put on platforms for others to develop.

INDUSTRY

When analyzing your organization's field of activities as a Building Block for your strategy, it is important to look into the type of industry you operate in, the pace of innovation in this industry, and how knowledge and IP are distributed.

1. TYPE OF INDUSTRY AND PACE OF INNOVATION

Firstly, it's important to take the type of industry into account; some industries take more easily to innovation and collaboration than others. The IT and food industries are fast-paced: there is pressure to constantly innovate to provide utility and keep users satisfied. This leads to a lot of competition in the industry itself. On the other hand, the air travel and real-estate industries are much slower. The most disruptive innovations in air travel were the collaboration of low-cost carriers with other travel service providers to offer comprehensive packages to travellers, and the concept of fractional ownership in private jets. Some industries place much more value on IP than others. For example, the IT industry has relatively more IP in play than the real-estate industry does.

2. DISTRIBUTION OF KNOWLEDGE

The environment in which your industry exists also plays a key role in how innovation takes place. In a calm environment, innovation evolves gradually and problems are clearly defined. In a more turbulent environment, there is much uncertainty: a variety of ideas will be competing to be at the forefront of unknown commercial applications[10]. Innovations may fundamentally change the market and may be disruptive. To an extent, this is also supported by the distribution of knowledge in your industry. Let's take the airline industry as an example again. There is a definite number of players, which means there are only so many possibilities for partnering, collaborating, or just exchanging ideas for

innovation. Conversely, in the IT industry, the number of industry players increases every day, leading to many sources of knowledge. This in turn results in a wide amount of industry-specific innovation.

3. DISTRIBUTION OF IP

An additional but equally important aspect is the distribution of IP in your industry. If all the IP is owned or being acquired by a few large players under strict licensing terms—or even worse: non-licensed— your organization will have to invest a lot of resources to secure its own position and compete. In case of several smaller players, there is a risk of unintentional infringement on other parties' IP, heavy costs for carrying out due-diligence, and high probabilities of litigation.

Bringing IP into play

➔ If the pace of innovation is very high in your industry, organizations may be less inclined to be very protective of their IP, or more open to sharing their IP. For example, the rate of innovation in digital technologies is quite high. The trend is for organizations to keep crucial or core IP to themselves, and share the rest openly in their ecosystems. If the pace of innovation is high and the core IP of the innovation is 'black-boxed' or kept as trade secrets, there is less pressure to patent everything and deal with the inherent administrative processes in patenting.

➔ If knowledge or IP is not distributed evenly across your industry, it may be better to collaborate with parties owning the knowledge or IP in order not to get behind. If you don't own the IP, you could also engage in activities like open-access research, or look into shielded innovation to work protectively with others.

➔ Sometimes, it can be better to build your own IP portfolio so as to avoid and manage potential litigation on infringement. On one hand, you can trace the origins of the IP under litigation (you can establish you had some related inventions/IP already) and underline the strength of your organization's IP portfolio. On the other hand, a worst-case scenario will mean you will have a host of related IP that can keep you going even if the courts don't favour you. (The next chapter covers all of these innovation models in more detail.)

"Failure
is an option here.
If things are not failing,
you are not
innovating enough."

—Elon Musk

Block
6

ORGANIZATION

SIZE, PACE, AGE

Last, but not least: consider your organization's characteristics and position in the ecosystem, its size, innovation culture, and company life cycle. Combined, these factors make up your organization's fingerprint. If your organization is a start-up, you will have to place larger importance on IP in order to attract investors, or find a way to expand your visibility in the ecosystem towards potential partners, customers, and suppliers.

As a mature organization, you will be in a position to nurture smaller organizations to grow within the ecosystem. Shell, IBM, Philips, and Johnson & Johnson play the role of foster parent to several organizations by licensing out their technology or even giving it away for free, or by providing infrastructure like labs to give them an opportunity to interact with the expertise in the ecosystem.

Tip

> The innovation attitude and culture in your organization is another factor that will largely sway the result of your activities. For more details, see Move 3: ACT.

Bringing IP into play

➡ If the **pace of innovation in your organization is higher** than that of your competitors and the industry in general, you can experiment more with your innovation and IP strategies. You might not even need to patent or protect your IP, as the rate at which you generate IP may keep you ahead of competition. However, this doesn't mean any IP will keep you ahead. A slow-paced innovator may be working on a ground-breaking technology, product, or service, which may suddenly launch that organization ahead of yours.

THINK *summary*

The analysis of these six Building Blocks helps you lay the foundation for your organization's innovation and IP strategy:

1. Interests Perspective of the owner, developer, or user / Joint, party-specific, or conflicting interests / Commercial, technical, and legal interests

2. Contribution Past or future investments (cash, in-kind, facilities, etc.) / Value of IP and know-how brought in / Channel to the market and networks

3. Technology Technology life cycle / Generic or specific technology / Segregability

4. Business model Technology needs a business model / Core vs. non-core business innovation

5. Industry Pace of innovation / Distribution of knowledge / Distribution of IP

6. Organization Size / Position in ecosystem and value chain / Innovation speed / Innovation attitude and culture / Life cycle

With the input you have gathered in this chapter, you can proceed to **MOVE 2: STRATEGIZE** where you can decide which innovation model and IP approach to apply to your case. **OR... CHECK OUT THE INFLUENCERS OF THE INNOVATION PROCESS IN THE NEXT SECTION.**

NEXT UP

STRATEGIZE

WAIT! WHERE DO THINGS GO WRONG?

While building an innovation and IP strategy is imperative, you cannot jump right into it without having a feeling for the approach you must take in the present–day world. In order to know how to do things right, you must also know where things go wrong—and how to overcome that. The three influencers identified in this section must be taken into account, as they will shape your approach.

Influencer #1
NO MAN IS AN ISLAND

Innovation today places a great deal of importance on relationship–building with the various parties involved in the innovation exercise. These parties can be your suppliers, your customers, or even your competitors. Similarly, these parties will also maintain relationships with others. This creates an interdependent and complex ecosystem within which several approaches to innovation and layers to a relationship can develop.

CONNECTION IS KEY

Companies like Airbnb or Facebook are well–known for always looking beyond money to seek value. Facebook Manager, Strategic Partnerships Ime Archibong famously quoted 'We want to make social companies big and big companies social.' In inquiring about how Facebook beat Google twice in acquiring Oculus and Whatsapp, Mark Zuckerberg mentions that he usually approaches big acquisitions by first forming friendships with the founders of the companies and sharing a vision; the other processes follow.

Such an approach is neither simple nor plain. A lot of thought goes into it. Ultimately, it feeds a larger commercial interest and acknowledges a certain degree of natural interdependency between companies: every relationship in the ecosystem has a cause–effect on the other relationships and on the growth of the ecosystem as a whole.

The relationship is not linear; there are several layers involved that make the different steps in the innovation process more complicated. The Facebook data breach in early 2018 shows the domino effect the trust layer had on its ecosystem: the very same ecosystem that grew by leaps and bounds because of the range of activities that Facebook offered is now being challenged.

SMART TAG HEUER

In 2015 a premium Swiss watch maker, Tag Heuer, partnered with Google and Intel to introduce luxury wearable technology. A seemingly odd combo, but here, Google was competing with Apple Watch, Intel was shifting from smartphones to watches, and Tag Heuer was leading the way with a luxury smartwatch, attracting the young and rich. We will leave you to ponder who made best use of this opportunity.

"IF YOU FEED THE NETWORK, THE NETWORK WILL FEED YOU."

—Peter Hinssen

DO: ENGAGE WITH YOUR NETWORK

Technology is increasingly important to the way business is conducted. Nevertheless, it is not unusual for a company to learn or utilize something from an entirely different industry. By not engaging with the network, your organization will risk missing out on opportunities or identifying risks.

Tip

Engaging with your ecosystem and forming trust-based relationships will enable you to reach not only for mutual, but also for cumulative benefits in the long run.

DON'T: MAKE A RELATIONSHIP PURELY TRANSACTIONAL

Today's new-age companies agree that if a partnership is purely transactional, it will fail. Innovation today is a trust-based, focused innovation process; it aims to create not just mutual benefits, but long-term cumulative benefits as well. There is a certain positive value attached to being in an ecosystem and making use of the network. Just as with social circles, business ecosystems increasingly exchange information, knowledge, and sometimes even resources, which are very much needed for survival in this competitive business world. When organizations fail to understand this, they may miss out on innovation solutions and opportunities, leading to failure.

Influencer #2
THE PARADOX OF OPENNESS

In order to innovate, companies often need to draw from, and collaborate with, a large number of actors from outside their organization. At the same time, companies need also to be focused on capturing the returns from their innovative ideas. This gives rise to a paradox of openness[11]: the creation of innovations often requires openness, but the commercialization of innovations requires protection.

YOU CANNOT SOLVE THE PARADOX OF OPENNESS,
BUT YOU CAN HANDLE IT.

DO: ASK THESE QUESTIONS

Each stage in the innovation process raises questions that need to be sufficiently addressed. The answers to these questions shape your IP strategy. Not answering them can thwart the development or innovation process and waste time, money, and resources. This is detrimental to the relationship between organizations.

☐ How can an organization's knowledge and IP be optimally distributed? How will the value in any existing future IP be determined?

☐ How will the IP contribution be evaluated?

☐ Who gets ownership? Who shares what?

☐ How will it be utilized?

☐ Do parties stick together or part ways at a certain stage?

☐ Who will market it?

☐ How will future IP value be captured and who will get the revenues?

☐ What options are available?

☐ How do you choose a suitable business model?

☐ Which model will bring sound value to the input and contribution made by each organization?

DON'T: JUST START—DETERMINE INTERESTS FIRST

Oftentimes, organizations sideline IP discussions and enthusiastically set out to work with innovation partners. Discussions about IP are perceived as a threat to the innovation process, because it is seen as thorny and time–consuming; it would slow down the speed and progress of innovation.

Organizations often believe IP can be dealt with when or after it is created. However, they may encounter a sudden breakdown in the relationship when the time comes to exploit and commercialize the innovation, since the parties involved have different expectations and interpretations on how IP is to be distributed amongst themselves. Parties should focus more on managing the interests and relationship of the parties involved, in order to turn their working together into a win–win situation.

HANDLE THE PARADOX

Can early IP discussion resolve the paradox of openness? No. However, it will mean you are better equipped to use IP not just as an asset, but also as a tool for your innovation route.

Influencer #3
THE MEDUSA EFFECT

Stringent IP policies prohibit communication between internal and external researchers[12]. V. Krishna and S.K. Jain call this the 'Medusa Effect'. We believe this effect to have an even wider connotation; it is not just IP policies which act as speed breakers—anything to do with IP in innovation might turn managers and business developers into stone!

FEAR IS A BAD ADVISOR

This reaction can be attributed to the often gruelling discussions with lawyers, both internally and externally. Some lawyers and innovation contracts are not flexible enough to adapt to the developments in an innovation process. Furthermore, standard terms and conditions cannot facilitate the multifaceted innovation process, or take into account innovation's various layers and needs at play. Not only does this place restrictions on the parties engaged in the innovation process, it can also hamper them in developing a fruitful relationship.

Tip

Don't allow yourself to turn into stone. You and your partners must realize that innovation is a multi faceted process that doesn't allow for standard terms and conditions lacking flexibility.

"IT IS NOT THE STRONGEST OF THE SPECIES THAT SURVIVES, NOR THE MOST INTELLIGENT, BUT THE ONE MOST RESPONSIVE TO CHANGE."

—Leon C. Megginson / Charles Darwin

STRATEGIZE

Gathering your innovation and IP options

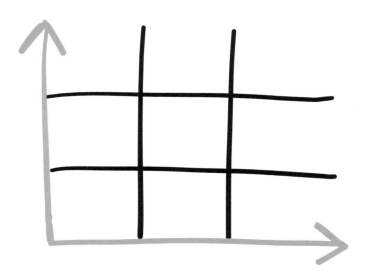

The Innovation and IP Matrix

	CLOSED		OPEN
REVEAL	FREE FOR PUBLIC	OPEN ACCESS RESEARCH	OPEN SOURCE
	LICENSING	COLLABORATIVE INNOVATION	CREATORS PLATFORM
GUARD	CLASSIC R & D	STEALTH INNOVATION	CROWD INNOVATION

This chapter focuses on finding your approach towards innovation partners and the IP in your innovation. We have identified an innovation and IP Matrix consisting of nine boxes. Each represents a strategy that will enable you to optimally capture the value of your innovation.

The first step was to analyze your business and innovation situation. Now it is time to determine an approach to capture the value of your innovation. Our innovation and IP Matrix is made up of small yet strategic boxes that help you find the right strategy to achieve your innovation goals.

THE MATRIX: INNOVATION APPROACH VS. CAPTURING VALUE

Our guide is represented as a matrix on two axes. The horizontal axis lays out the innovation approach you take towards your partners —ranging from Closed to Open—and determines how you will work with them. The vertical axis lays out the approach towards capturing the value of innovation or its IP—ranging from Guard to Reveal—and determines what you do with the IP related to your innovation.

Based on the axes, the Matrix is made up of nine boxes that can represent strategies for your innovation and the IP involved in it. The four corners are fixed strategies. For example, at one extreme (Closed & Guarded), you may choose to do classic R&D, where any innovation happens within the walls of your organization. Here, your business model may just be to sell off a product or service, while at the other extreme (Open & Reveal), you may choose to work freely with many partners and reveal all details about your innovation publicly. Here, you may fish for ideas from third parties, develop your technology or product further before selling it or let others build on your core innovation.

In between these extremes are creative strategies you can craft for your innovation. In this section, we will take you through the four fixed strategies and five examples of what could be creative in-betweens.

Tip

HOW TO USE THE MATRIX

The Matrix is not rigid. An organization may have more than one strategy, and strategies do not necessarily have to fit exactly into a single box. What may work for one business, industry, product, or technology may not work for another. However, with these Building Blocks in mind, you can determine your needs, and dos and don'ts. Once that is clear, you can step into the Matrix. This step is meant to reduce complexity, provide structure, and help you better understand your innovation setting and options.

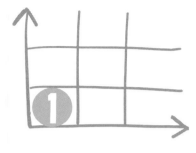

CLASSIC R&D

In case of classic R&D, parties innovate on their own and keep their knowledge closely guarded.

It may come as a surprise, but Apple—one of the world's most popular innovators—practices this classic closed innovation strategy[1]. The best people work for Apple, they do not engage in open forum or press discussions, there is very little or no information available about the product they are working on until its release. Apple is also very sceptic about sharing their IP.

Bringing IP into play

→ You can think of many Building Blocks that come into play here. We assume some of the key elements are Apple's technology, innovation culture (organization) and, more importantly, the chosen business model for their products. At the same time, it offers a great deal of potential for open innovation through their App Store. This is a playground for several developers who function in their own ecosystem. Here, they seem to have taken into account the interests of users and developers, ascribing more importance to their contributions. They tap into the distributed knowledge of others, as you will also see in some cases below. Apple, thus, spreads across two boxes: Classical R&D and the Creators' Platform.

FREE FOR THE PUBLIC

This is one of the strategies where innovation happens in a classic R&D set-up, and yet the results are made freely available to the public[2]. In 2015, Toyota opened up their patents on hydrogen technology for others until 2020 without a royalty fee. While this is free, it is not open to all. Toyota wants to let others develop hydrogen cells, hybrid car products, etc. to boost the ecosystem. Car manufacturers, engineering companies and such can apply for access and on a case–by–case basis; Toyota decides who receives the free IP.

Bringing IP into play

→ Companies often choose this strategy in order to boost another part of the business or even the whole ecosystem with IP that is in a later phase of the technology life cycle. This approach is often applied in case of common or joint interests between the parties involved or within the ecosystem. Time influences IP and its connection to the ecosystem; IP that was developed in a classical environment by one party may over time be used in new applications or become of renewed importance due to new reasoning, trends, or third–party motives. Interestingly enough, some organizations freely give away what they do, but not always how they do it.

FREE FOR THE PUBLIC (CONT'D)

Sometimes, providing access to an organization's IP can bring in more benefits or returns on related products, rather than selling that particular product—and protecting its IP—at a high price. The Building Blocks at play combine an organization's business model with ways to boost the relevant industry's ecosystem and the shared interests of the parties. Sometimes, the combination also includes capturing value for products or services almost at the end of their technology life cycle.

TESLA

It is Elon Musk's vision that it would actually be good if Tesla had some more competition, as it would help grow his business[4]. Tesla's key competition is still the traditional automotive industry. Tesla's goal and interest is populating the world with battery stations to fuel the future of their electric cars—a truly massive task. If it can stir up massive 'competitors' to partner with, existing infrastructure issues would be greatly reduced. In order to spur more competitors and build the ecosystem, a major part of Tesla's IP is not held defensively. They are patented, but freely available, as long as they are used for 'good' i.e. they are in line with Tesla's vision. This is a true and new example of parties providing free access to their R&D results/IP in order to boost the ecosystem, business model, or product sales.

In this case, Tesla utilizes the shared interest of the electric car manufacturers ecosystem, and opens up an IP portfolio that was built and kept secret for a long time. In a way, they seek to encourage the distribution of IP to strengthen their future business model. Moreover, by doing so, they are also tapping into the resources of other developers by giving them a foundation technology. It is debatable whether they would have taken this approach if the technology had been more advanced.

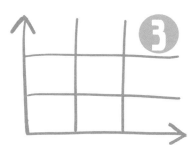

OPEN SOURCE

Parties openly collaborate to develop knowledge, software, etc. granting everybody open access and permission to use it. Linux is a co-created product; thousands of contributors build and enhance the product and everyone benefits. Its large Open Source community produces vastly more software than a proprietary competitor, and shares in the production and go-to-market costs.

The Open Source box often combines several Building Blocks. Parties may open up their business model to attract contribution, to expand the field of use, or to develop a technology further, but most often do so because their developers and/or users share an interest in growing as a collective. Some organizations even open up the non-core IP within their business model to stimulate the sale of other core products. When the innovation and its IP become specific and mature, organizations may choose to split up to continue innovating the product or service individually. Consider the technology Building Block; at the start of the technology life cycle, while parties are developing more embryonic IP, there is often a shared interest to grow as a collective. When the IP becomes specific and product-related, parties split up and continue individually.

Bringing IP into play

→ This strategy is often combined with other innovation strategies such as classical R&D, or adopted entirely to support the notion of 'common good for all'. It is a strategy that also allows others to contribute. You might think an Open Source approach can only work with software and that Open Source is always free, but you would be wrong. In recent years, a tremendous number of hardware-centric organizations and communities have adopted the Open Source approach. The Air Quality Egg is both an Open Source, internet of things pollution monitor and a marketable device. The device is described as a building block for innovations, thereby opening it up to many more possibilities than originally envisaged. WikiHouse is another example: the project seeks to democratize the way houses are built and offers downloadable building plans. What's in it for them? Common good!

EXAMPLE

FACEBOOK

"Facebook is built on Open Source from top to bottom, and could not exist without it[6]". Further, Facebook's Open Compute invites the world to not just build a data centre in Facebook's image, but to extend it and improve upon it. From networking switches to designs for servers, power systems, storage and cooling equipment; they want to create an Open Source data centre. Facebook writes and contributes a great |deal of incredibly useful software. They are also an active contributor to industry-defining Open Source projects like Apache Hadoop, MySQL, and PHP. Businesses such as these see competitive advantage in giving away code without restricting access to it, so others can develop it further and add more value to the collective. With the gradual move to a sharing economy, other, similar businesses will most likely follow suit in the near future.

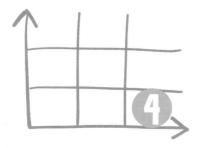

CROWD INNOVATION
Parties openly invite the public to solve a problem. Sometimes, this will involve specific instructions. In some cases, participants are eligible for prizes or royalties; in return, the organizer captures some or all of the value and/or IP. It could be a relatively simple, inexpensive, and fast way to generate ideas.

Bringing IP into play

→ Crowd innovation—involving the general public to solve an issue or create something new—is sometimes considered risky, since it may lead to chaos beforehand. But if you accept that knowledge is widespread, then **approaching crowds is a way of tapping into potent geniuses**. One of the reasons crowds are a great source for innovation is that crowds have various drivers that make them come up with brilliant ideas. Many people and teams worldwide are enthusiastic about submitting ideas to organizations to get recognition, be a part of a community or a brand, compete for a prize, or receive a small licence fee in return. Here, too, you can get very creative with IP. You can gain a lot of IP from crowd submissions, or you can just pick ideas to sharpen and develop internally, or identify a problem to which you may already have a solution.

These examples are an interesting blend of an interests-based business model and organization-based IP distribution. LEGO users await a new play experience, and letting them participate in the innovation process is a way to share and distribute each side's interests. LEGO also does not stray very far from their core business to innovate, instead sticking to a clearly defined business model. LEGO also seems to have worked on their collaboration mindset by doing a turnaround within the organization. Collaborating outside the organization was another step. LEGO capitalized greatly on innovation methods, even when faced with adversity like the Mindstorms hacking (see next page). As a result, they managed to completely turn around their earlier decline.

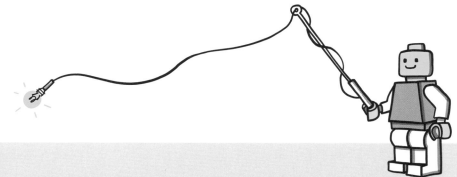

EXAMPLE

LEGO

LEGO was a product of innovation that originated in a carpenter's shed around the 1910s. Over the years, children and adults have indulged in creating several play experiences using simple bricks, but all was not simple for this business. The late 90s and early 2000s saw a decline to which LEGO management responded with an innovation spree. This period was one of unfocused innovation, where the costs exceeded the results brought in. Gradually, LEGO started focusing their innovation efforts on their core business.

In 1988, 'LEGO's robotics platform, created with MIT's Media Lab, gave the Future Lab some of its key DNA. It was the company's first hybrid digital physical experience, and was the first time adult fans were brought into the design process.'[8] 'Within three weeks after Mindstorms was launched, more than one thousand advanced users had hacked into the software that came with the construction toys to make unauthorized modifications with new functions. These designs were completely original and unforeseen by the company. Within a short space of time, the hackers had vastly improved the original product which resulted in many more units being sold—particularly to customers over the age of 18, who were not LEGO's target market'[9]. Even though the core product was developed by software engineers from MIT, the crowd-sourced innovation was beyond any possibilities foreseen by LEGO. Despite initial management opposition, LEGO realized that their most hardcore users knew more about programming toys than they did[10].

In 2011, LEGO introduced 'LEGO Ideas', which took open innovation through crowdsourcing to the next level. Under this program, 'fans [voted] on new-kit ideas submitted by amateur designers. Anything with more than ten thousand votes [went] to a review phase, and LEGO [decided] which [got] made. So far, the process has created more than ten limited-availability kits, including a model lab staffed by female scientists and the Big Bang Theory apartment'[11]. As far as IP distribution goes, the authorship on the new design is credited to the fan, who receives 1 per cent of the profit on the sales of the new product. LEGO has several innovation strategies, both open and closed. However, the key takeaways from their success and failures are on how they aligned their business strategy and their IP strategy with their core context.

NOKIA AND AIRBUS FISH FOR IDEAS

The Nokia Open Innovation Challenge organizes yearly hunts for futuristic tech, ideas, and new business models in the Internet of things (IoT) domain. Airbus works with start-ups through its BizLab accelerator, and provides support to help mature innovative concepts that they can use later on, through their existing platforms. These organizations search for ideas to improve their product/service, new talent, or more interest among their community. Whatever the reason, it is a great strategy to stimulate a community.

the mellow middle of
THE INNOVATION PLUS

The centre of our Matrix is fluid. An organization can take several approaches to innovation in these middle areas, by deviating from the extremes identified earlier to the extent necessary for their case. In this section, you will find some examples to give you an idea of the possibilities the middle strategies provide.

LICENSING

A licence is a legal agreement in which an IP owner ('licensor') grants a third party ('licensee') certain rights to use their IP. Sometimes, in order to boost revenues on past innovation investments, parties license their IP to others.

There are several ways to create licences. Samsung for instance needs licences from Motorola and Apple to manufacture smartphones. Since the other companies also need licences, they end up granting cross-licences[12]. The core Building Block here is interests: these organizations need each other's IP to manufacture their own products without infringing on the other parties. Delving deeper into this example shows that these companies also engage in classical R&D or collaborative innovation with other parties, through which they own valuable IP that they can put into the cross-licensing pool.

"The more you share
the more you get."

The
WEDDING CAKE MODEL

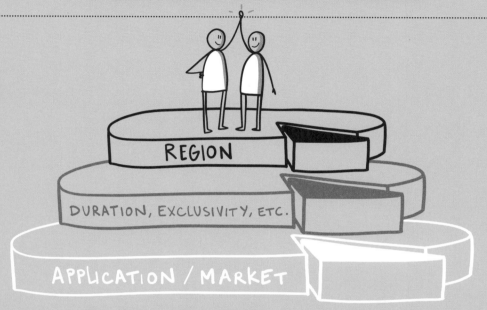

One of our favourite tools within licensing is the Wedding Cake model[13] of IP distribution. IP is seen here as a bundle of rights. These rights can be isolated into three tiers that will distinguish between fields for IP distribution: Geographical Region, Duration, Exclusivity etc., and Application/Market. Within each of these tiers, the licensor can also apply an additional tier that deals with exclusivity. This is essentially a licensing mechanism that defines where or in what context the IP is used: where the licensee can exploit the IP, the field of use for its commercial exploitation or a combination of rights that includes an exploitation time–limit.

The advantage of using the Wedding Cake model is that the same innovation can be distributed in several creative ways to several parties instead of licensing the complete innovation to only one party. The organization's business model plays a pivotal role here, too. For example, when a business aims to prioritize business development in Asia and disinvest in South America, it is logical to distribute IP limited in geographic application or utility. Before you unleash your creativity in using this model, you will have to evaluate your need for the 'freedom to operate': which field are you active in now, what is core and non–core regarding technology and market, and where do you want to be active in the future? Again, if you do not have an innovation strategy, these questions are hard to answer, making it difficult to apply the Wedding Cake model. Any Building Block from the earlier section can be of great help in this stage.

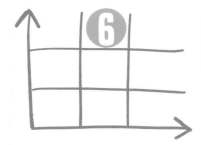

OPEN ACCESS RESEARCH

With a common objective, parties come together to boost existing knowledge, share ideas, and engage in new development. Parties may sometimes be required to pay a fee for coming together and gaining access to each other's knowledge.

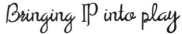

Bringing IP into play

→This strategy is used when organizations want to gain more insight into and/or influence on research agendas in order to learn about the progress and direction of the research, contribute to it, and reap the benefits. It is especially interesting to use this strategy in environments where innovation costs are high and/or the pace of innovation is high. If it is applied to a generic part of the technology life cycle, commercial organizations can build on these innovations for their more specific technology and product developments through a more classical R&D approach.

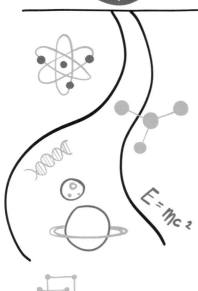

EXAMPLE
HORIZON EUROPE

Horizon 2020 is the biggest EU Research and Innovation programme ever, spanning seven years (2014 to 2020). Its aim is to engage the EU community in research and innovation to produce world-class science, remove barriers to innovation, and make it easier for the public and private sectors to innovate together. Funded by the EU, the programme contains contributions from private participants and works towards a common goal, with all involved pooling their expertise. All parties have access to each other's knowledge to fulfil the objectives. Parties are also obliged to share their findings or results openly with the EU community to promote further innovation and research. Should they want to commercialize the results of their innovation, there is guidance on how to allocate financially, contractually and technically between parties. This is a great example of how to promote innovation at an institutional level through open access research. However, in order to be able to define the best way forward regarding IP, parties will first need to analyze their situation and opportunities properly.

In terms of Building Blocks, the purpose of such regional initiatives—apart from shared interests—is to distribute knowledge in a field to positively influence and spur innovation both within the innovation collective and beyond it. Such a strategy may also be used to channel contributions. In that case, parties pool more than just money and subsidies; they also have a pool of knowledge at their disposal.

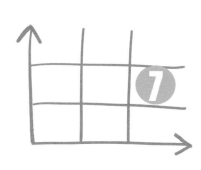
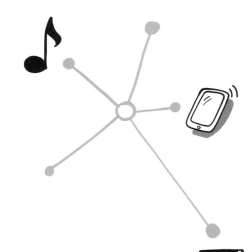

CREATORS' PLATFORM

In this model, parties provide access to a standardized platform on which other parties can develop and sell their own service/product. The platform owner gets a fee in return, and/or can use the platform as a market place.

Building Blocks at play here are the pace of innovation and contribution. By letting others add value to the organization's IP, the organization benefits from added value without huge investments—increase in sales, fees from developers and users, etc. In a way, this model allows app developers to expand the market for core product and services as well. Since the app developers have extensive expertise regarding end customers and user experiences, they also contribute to enhancing the marketing channel of a product, technology, and/or service.

Bringing IP into play

→When they choose this option, innovators also become networkers: they connect two settings/categories of people through a platform. For example, you may be engaging in classical R&D within your organization, but see that different groups of people (students, developers, businesses) can make different contributions to what you have, or add more value through their use. The ideal way to capture value in such a case would be through a creators' platform. On the one hand, you protect what you have, but on the other, you make part of the process available to particular groups, so they can benefit from their value addition. This is smart use of the network effect.

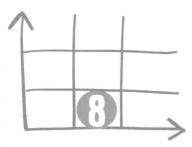

STEALTH INNOVATION

Stealth Innovation means going under the radar. The innovation or development is secret and kept under wraps until a certain point of time or a certain maturity is reached, either externally and internally. In case of external stealth innovation, parties invite others to develop together in undercover mode. Parties do not disclose their strategic innovations to competitors or the outside world. It is a way to speed up the pace of innovation without revealing the companies' objectives and technology, thereby protecting their interests and a possible business model.

The internal variant of this model is to go under the radar within the organization itself, for example when a generated idea is considered viable, but will have to clear a lot of red tape. Sometimes this may kill the idea itself, so this is both a survival mechanism and a gamble. Parties can innovate within their own organization with a few selected partners.

EXAMPLE
PFIZERWORKS

A single Pfizer employee created a productivity initiative that allows employees to outsource 'grunt work' and routine parts of their jobs, giving them more time to focus on important tasks and allowing Pfizer to make better use of their highly skilled (and highly paid) employees. PfizerWorks, launched in 2008, quickly became an acknowledged success story. However, this innovation was under the radar for over a year before it was brought to the top execs for approval.

Bringing IP into play

→External stealth innovation requires complementary competences and/or technologies, but the organization doesn't want to reveal the area of innovation. Internal stealth innovation is controversial and sometimes seen as toxic to an organization.

"UNFORTUNATELY,
NO ONE CAN BE TOLD
WHAT THE MATRIX IS.
YOU HAVE TO SEE
IT FOR YOURSELF."

—"Morpheus" (Laurence Fishburne), The Matrix

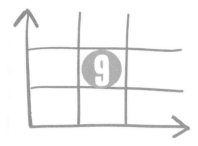

COLLABORATIVE INNOVATION

Collaborative innovation is an umbrella term that encompasses varying degrees of collaboration, in other words: different parties working together on the same or a similar innovation activity. In this section, we will discuss three common possibilities. Collaborative innovation includes but is not limited to collaborative open licensing, the shield approach, and selective revealing.

A. COLLABORATIVE OPEN LICENSING

Shared information and technology leads to the creation of reciprocal value and IP. If someone's background info is used, the foreground is licensed to all (see the definitions of these terms on page 101). This means participants in the innovation activity openly share ideas, information, and/or technology. Each participant may get an open licence or access to another parties input. And where there is sharing, there is reciprocity. The Holst Centre case (page 37) is an example of such collaborative innovation.

For example, if X uses Y's background info, X gives something back to Y. If X, Y, and Z use A's background technology and create something new, A may receive reciprocal benefits in that A can have some rights to use the technology developed by X,Y, and Z, and so on.

B. SHIELD

In industries with an increased risk of IP litigation, parties join to form a consortium that holds and manages a collective IP portfolio, or work with an organization that manages IP portfolios. The consortium or IP management organization will identify critical patents that create a significant risk of liability and infringement, which will be acquired and protected for the parties in the consortium, or for clients of the IP management organization. This defensive method is preferred to protect organizations from litigation, and critical inventions from having to face hindrances from patent trolls who would obtain patents purely for asserting IP claims and licensing.

A party can choose to share its knowledge selectively to its partners or compartmentalize its knowledge, so partners work together on a 'need-to-know' basis only. In other to keep the innovation closely guarded, they never reveal the full picture.

EXAMPLE
LINDT & SPRÜNGLI CHOCOLATE

With over a century's worth of knowledge in the chocolate industry, Lindt & Sprüngli's strategy [14] is a prime example of how the old reacts to the new. Lindt & Sprüngli follows a selective revealing method in innovation that boils the entire industrial process down into four elements. Concept, recipe, packaging, and machinery are compartmentalized and the flow of information is controlled. 'In the area of flavours, for example, Lindt has developed an elaborate system of collaboration based on a list of preferred suppliers for each type of flavour, the company works using an iterative procedure until the suitable blend is obtained' [15].
They employ a mix of the interests and the Wedding Cake model where the exchange of information is subject to several boundaries. IP, both registered and unregistered, is then controlled and monitored, where any resultant rights are well-defined and distributed at a very early stage.

Definition
SELECTIVE REVEALING

Selective revealing [16] is a method that allows organizations sceptical of openness to benefit by choosing to share information or knowledge of limited value only, or to limit the number of parties with whom it is being shared.

Bringing
IP into play

→ This is the most creative and diverse box in the Matrix. It's an umbrella term for several ways of collaborating (and distributing IP) with partners. Maybe your organization applies a different kind of collaborative innovation. There are many more options than the three we have mentioned. Further research will have to uncover other approaches and possibilities for this segment.

Before you get going with the Tools in MOVE 3: ACT, you might want to dive a little deeper into the opportunities of the platform business model.

Platform business model
A NEW METHOD FOR BUSINESS AND INNOVATION

At the turn of the century, with the internet percolating into our world, we saw a paradigm shift in how we create, consume and interact with the rest of the world. We have come to accept a sharing or access economy, where the use of products/services is of more value than 'ownership'. Technology too, particularly in the use of software, pervaded most organizations. This challenged traditional pipeline business models and resulted in the evolution of the 'platform business model'.

A PLATFORM TRANSACTION IN 4 STEPS

To an old soul, this is very similar to what happens in auction houses:

1. There is a place.
2. There is a mediator who connects the owner of some antique mahogany wardrobe or a pair of skates, to potential buyers.
3. The auctioneer taps into their network to get both parties together.
4. At the end of the transaction, both the buyer and the seller would pay a transaction fee to the auctioneer... for providing a platform to connect!

EXPLORING THE PLATFORM BUSINESS MODEL

Contrary to the pipeline model, in which products and services are aimed towards a singular target group, the platform business model has two or more sides connecting creators, consumers, contributors, and sometimes even more parties. The platform taps into and works within an ecosystem to enable an exchange. Although the platform's core value is in the technology or software that enables this exchange, it should not be considered merely a piece of technology or software. The several layers to the technology—including but not limited to the ecosystem, products/services traded, interactions within its network, etc.—make it an indispensable business model in today's technology-driven world. Top businesses in the world, such as Google and Facebook, capitalize on the platform business model. However, technology companies are not the only ones taking this path. Formerly traditional transactional businesses also use this model: Alibaba, LEGO, Philips Lighting, etc. have found success either by adopting the platform business model entirely, or for a select number of their products/services.

THE CLASSICAL PIPELINE MODEL

 PRODUCTION
 DISTRIBUTION
 MARKETING
 CONSUMERS

SANGEET PAUL CHOUDARY IN WWW.WIRED.COM/INSIGHTS/2013/10/WHY-BUSINESS-MODELS-FAIL-PIPES-VS-PLATFORMS/

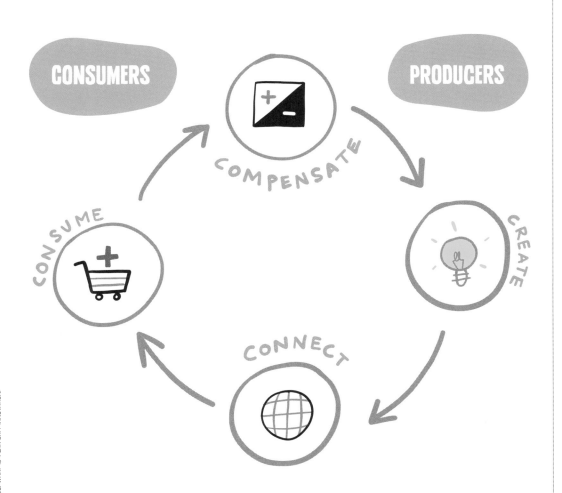

THE PLATFORM BUSINESS MODEL IN SHORT

Alex Moazed, founder of platform innovation company Applico, describes the platform model concisely as 'a business model that creates value by facilitating exchanges between two or more interdependent groups, usually consumers and producers. In order to make these exchanges happen, platforms harness and create large, scalable networks of users and resources that can be accessed on demand.'

Platform business model

EXAMPLE

LEGO AGAIN

As we have seen earlier, LEGO uses a creators' platform to invite ideas for new LEGO sets. They offer recognition and one percent sale proceeds to creators whose sets are approved. LEGO makes use of a third-party idea, captures its IP value to further their own business, while engaging their users to vote for new set ideas. They provide a winning incentive to creators and in turn, they drive more activity within the 'community'.

EXAMPLE

YOUTUBE

YouTube is another platform business that connects media content providers to media consumers. YouTube monetizes customer attention by placing advertisements along content. Over time, a new business evolved within this platform: some content is now available on demand—for a fee. For example, instead of paying €12 to watch the Minions movie, we can simply watch it on demand for €3. A user who uploads content on YouTube can opt for a 'Standard Licence', giving YouTube users the right to use and broadcast the video—sometimes in exchange for a percentage of any advertising revenues—or a 'Creative Commons Licence', which expands on the SL by extending the rights of use to any other consumer, in addition to the Standard Licence.

MONETIZING THE PLATFORM

The advantages of embracing this business model are manifold. It is a dynamic model that enables organizations to enlarge their base or expand the range of their exchanges. For example, Twitter started off as a platform to share your 'thoughts' with your network in 140 characters. Over time, it has developed into a consumer's platform for updates and breaking news. Most platforms also tap into the services of big data analytics to gather business intelligence about the use of their platform, which they use to further optimize their platform.

Moreover, there are several ways to structure and monetize the platform, depending on your organizational needs. Usually, both the platform provider and consumer feel like they're in a win–win situation. One way to do that is through providing a subsidy, in exchange for something that is of non-monetary business value. Facebook may provide their social networking platform for free to a few billion users, but they also earn money from advertisers and app developers who use the Facebook platform to easily reach those same several billion people.

A GREATER IMPACT

Global e-commerce giants Alibaba and Amazon—catering to B2B and B2C needs respectively—have taken marketplace transactions to a whole new level with the range of their network and the services they offer both providers and consumers. Apart from the standard exchanges in a platform business, these businesses have a larger socio-economic impact: Amazon Prime's delivery policies have become part of daily life in developed countries and Alibaba's easy payment mechanisms have facilitated larger volumes of transactions. There is no transfer of IP in these businesses. However, the different elements of the platform itself, like Alibaba's payment mechanisms, are proprietary knowledge.

PHILIPS HUE

Philips Lighting applies intuitive technology to LED lights. These lights can be controlled by a smartphone app to set the ambience, create home safety propositions, or adapt the light to functional needs. Philips Hue calls their collaborators 'Friends of Hue'. Their ecosystem consists of leading companies, such as Amazon, Apple, Google, Samsung, etc. that all interface with the Philips Hue lighting system in some way, each adding some value to the user experience.

The ecosystem's functional base consists of an API (Application Programming Interface) and an SDK (Software Development Kit) that can be utilized by developers generating new apps and thereby adding cases to the Hue proposition. For example, a photographer who would like to pre-program mood lighting for various portraits can develop a specialized app that will benefit other photographers too, and share this with the Philips Hue community.

This is a remarkable shift to the platform model for a particular product. Allowing others to customize a product will not have been an easy choice for the originally pipeline-based Philips Lighting. Nevertheless, it is a grand success. With positive user feedback, which is common to platform businesses, drives up demand so both the producer and reap the consumer benefits. The community of users and app developers has expanded since the product launch, enabling them to customize the lights and enhance the proposition. This may also increase producer revenue. But how does it work in terms of IP? Who owns what? The Philips Hue developers' website contains a small paragraph that addresses these questions. *See excerpt below:*

"Free to publish"

'Philips has a quite progressive policy with hue. As you are free to create with our product, we think it should also be you who profits from your work. What you produce you own and are free to give away or sell. There's a little catch—this also means that everything connected with use of your product is your responsibility. Philips will not accept liability if your product causes harm, for example. So use your powers for good! And, it's up to you whether and on what terms you choose to commercialize your prod-

uct. So while we say "what is yours is yours", on the flip side we also say, "what is ours is ours". Here, we mean the software, trademarks documentation, and any other materials we provide to help you develop hue apps. For example, you may refer to "hue" and "Philips" in plain text but you aren't allowed to use "hue" or "Philips" branding in any logo or graphics. Also important to note is that the interface specifications "API" belong to Philips. Imagine you are working on an app and you come up with a brilliant idea

for an improvement in the API or our materials. If you suggest any improvements to us and we adopt them, they become part of the platform used by everyone, and will belong to us.

Oh, a little aside on UI (User Interface): as the interface between your apps and the hue platform will evolve over time, we will do our level best to maintain backwards compatibility and will inform you with enough time, before we roll out updates. That's why, to keep everyone up to date, we ask you to register your apps [...].'

DISTRIBUTION OF IP IN THE
Platform business model

In the previous examples, you may have noticed that when looking at platforms through IP-tinted glasses, they generally tend to fall into one of two categories. Keep in mind that the platform model doesn't suit every business, but that some of its elements may prove useful to kick–start your strategy.

① NO IP IS INVOLVED

The platform is purely transactional; products or services move from the provider to the consumer. The platform is merely the orchestrator that connects the parties, whereas the provider and consumer will transfer a product or service in exchange for some remuneration. Alibaba and Amazon are examples of orchestrator platforms.

② IP IS INVOLVED TO DIFFERENT DEGREES

This second category deals with IP or its derivatives in various forms and to various extent. In our examples, you may have noticed that YouTube, LEGO, and Philips Hue deal with a significant exchange of IP or its derivatives. Users uploading content to YouTube must give the platform a licence to distribute and use it. LEGO taps into the creativity of their users to build a new model set. They acquire the idea; in exchange, they credit the creator and give them an incentive. Similarly, Philips Hue expands the uses for their lighting system by allowing developers to identify these uses. Think back to the Building Blocks and innovation model from the previous section, and you will have no difficulty judging their business strategy. In these cases, although not visibly, IP is used as a tool within their business strategy.

STRATEGIZE
summary

The Innovation and IP Matrix helps you determine an approach towards finding the right innovation partners and capturing the value of your innovation and the IP in it. It represents a framework of 9 strategies.

....

1. These strategies vary on a scale of open vs. closed innovation and guarding vs. revealing IP: classic R&D, free for the public, Open Source, crowd innovation, licensing, open access research, collaborative innovation, stealth innovation, and creators' platform.

....

2. The strategies can be used in various permutations and combinations. The trick is to use several strategies for your business model instead of sticking with one approach for everyone and every product/service.

....

3. In terms of licensing, you can use the Wedding Cake model as a tool to help you distribute IP creatively to several parties. It is a licensing mechanism that defines where or in what context the IP is used.

....

4. Traditional pipeline business models are being challenged. This has resulted in the rise of the platform business model. A platform model doesn't suit every business, but some of its elements may provide any strategy with new impulses.

 NEXT UP  **ACT**

move

3

ACT

Strategy implementation

The IP Toolbox

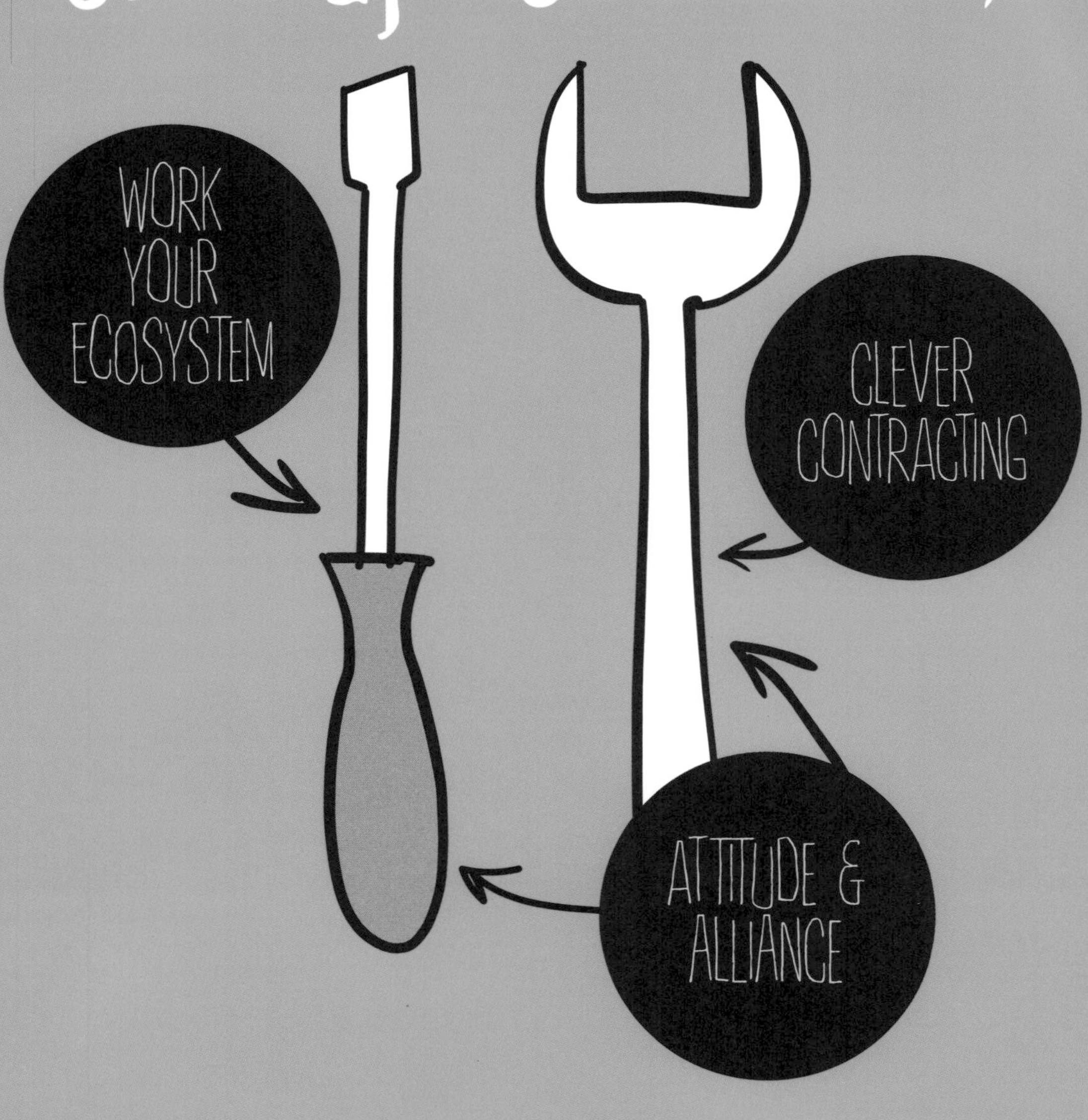

Upcycled Tools for the new world

In this section, we will introduce three Tools that you can use to implement your strategy: working your ecosystem, clever contracting, and the right attitude.

A t this stage, you may have a draft strategy for your innovation case. How do you implement this strategy? In this chapter, we will introduce three prerequisites that will help you implement the strategy and help you achieve your innovation ambitions. These Tools are not new, they are just upcycled! Your organization and the people you work with might very well be aware of these Tools, but are they making the most of them?

"WE ARE FINALLY IN A STATE OF CO-CONTROL."

–Daan Roosegaarde

WORK YOUR ECOSYSTEM: TURN ON THE CHARM!

Back in the day, railroads contributed to a nation's economy by transporting workers and moving raw materials to and from factories. Gradually, it facilitated settlement and boosted commerce. Communities were built around prime railroad centres and more markets were created for the products from factories. This was the ripple effect railroads caused on the economy; connectivity lead to the formation of an ecosystem, which in turn lead to the growth and development of a nation.

ASK YOURSELF SOME QUESTIONS

Greatness on your part is not enough. You are no longer an autonomous innovator; you are an actor within a broader innovation ecosystem[1]. Do you know your ecosystem? What do you contribute to it? How do you benefit from it? If you are unable to give definite answers, you are not connected! How then does your organization grow and develop?

In today's world, every organization needs to be connected to others in its industry and beyond in order to thrive in business, meet challenges, and keep up with the competition. Being part of an ecosystem will facilitate interactions, as well as help identify opportunities and challenges, trends and risks. Most importantly, it will help you build connections. To be part of the ecosystem and benefit from its dynamics, you simply have to be responsive to it.

IS THE ECOSYSTEM READY?

Imagine that your organization is creating the coolest innovation of the year. If your ecosystem is not ready for it, it will fail—no matter how cool it is. In the late 1990s, Hollywood decided to bring digital cinema to America's movie theatres. They rolled it out in 1999, with the blockbuster release of *Star Wars: Episode I–The Phantom Menace*. Seven years later, a mere 5 percent of the nation's screens were using digital projection. Why? The studios hadn't confronted the conversion costs for theatres: upward of $70,000 per screen for all the necessary hardware and software. Finally, Hollywood recognized its failing, found a way to subsidize the theatres' adoption of the technology, and it took off[2].

"BE MINDFUL OF THE FUTURE, BUT NOT AT THE EXPENSE OF THE MOMENT".

— *Star Wars: Episode I*

WHO ARE THE ACTORS IN THE ECOSYSTEM?

The ecosystem for innovation will broadly consist of actors from the knowledge economy and the commercial economy[3], i.e. the typical ecosystem for innovation may include business organizations, universities, the government, funding agencies, research institutes, customers, users, and even competitors—each working on its own interests. Nevertheless, their work may have an impact on your organization, so it is important to interact with these actors to help identify opportunities and challenges, trends, and risks.

HAVE YOU MAPPED THEIR INTERESTS?

Even if your ecosystem is indeed ready for your innovation, you will go down the slippery slope of failure if you don't play an active role in it, or if you are not sensitive to the dynamics and interests of your ecosystem. When Sony brought out the revolutionary 'Reader' for e-books, they did not take into the account the actors in their eco-system—authors and publishers—pushing the device to somewhat of a failure. On the other hand, Amazon managed to successfully turn things around with their relatively inferior 'Kindle': they set up an online store for e-books and offered a wide variety of books, making it a go-to place for readers. It also supported self-published authors by connecting reviewers etc., and managed digital rights by taking into account the interests of parties in the ecosystem, making it a success.

WHAT DO ACTORS NEED FROM EACH OTHER?

Actors in the ecosystem have different relationships with one another. What does that relationship enable? What is its purpose?

Interact with diverse parties, form new connections, and open channels for connectivity.

Resources to share and utilize.

Involve the right people in innovation activities, including attracting new talent.

Exchange and test ideas and knowledge.

Create a strong feedback loop.

Nurture the network.

STAKEHOLDER MAPPING

Relationships between actors will not necessarily be similar. You can establish each relationship based on the Building Blocks in Move 1. Then, when you zoom out, you can see how your ecosystem is structured. The sum of all relationships determines how your organization will collaborate and innovate.

SUPPORT NETWORKS

... ?

INVESTORS

POLICY MAKERS

YOU

FUNDING AGENCIES

GOVERNMENT BODIES

CUSTOMERS

ACADEMIA

RESEARCH INSTITUTES

COMMUNITY

PARTNERS

SUPPLIERS

USERS

HAIER'S HOPE: TECHNOLOGY SCOUTING

Consumer electronics company, Haier's HOPE (Haier Open Partnership Ecosystem), is a perfect example of how you can benefit from an ecosystem. HOPE's website states that it: 'provides professional technology scouting and technology transfer services'. By getting access to these brilliant minds outside of your company, you will be able to solve technical problems, break development bottlenecks, and find technologies faster and more efficiently. In addition, you can promote and commercialize your technology here. The mission of HOPE is 'to maximize the outcomes for all parties.'[4]

In HOPE, Haier found a solution to a problem in refrigeration. While Haier was looking for a solution to address a lack of a low-humidity 'dry zone' to protect fragile produce such as mushrooms, HOPE helped it to connect to the China Paper Research Institute (CPRI). This unusual partner provided an adapted solution it had developed for some other purpose, making CPRI Haier's supplier later on[5].

In terms of IP, HOPE uses several strategies depending on how the collaboration is structured: IP can be acquired from, shared, or pooled, amongst collaborators. HOPE helps broaden Haier's communications channel with an ever-increasing range of solution providers including consumers themselves, creating significant competitive advantage in an industry with notoriously challenging market conditions.[6]

With big players like Apple, Google, Tesla etc. recognizing the merits of working in an ecosystem, more organizations are moving towards this approach and reaping its benefits.

CLEVER CONTRACTING

Innovation in the VUCA world is not easy. To avoid innovation apocalypses, organizations must cope with business Volatility, Uncertainty, Complexity and Ambiguity in various stages of the innovation process, particularly when collaborating with other parties. You may have built a marvellous innovation and IP strategy for your innovation projects, but you will need smart and flexible contracting in order to successfully implement the strategy and reach your objective.

The most common hurdle in getting to an agreement between innovation collaborators is that some organizations use boilerplate, protective terms and conditions for all innovation projects. When you consider of the 'paradox of openness', using boilerplate will protract negotiations and threaten opportunities for innovation, the organization's reputation as a collaborator, relationships in the ecosystem, and eventually the innovation's commercial success. Even worse is sidelining contract and IP discussions in a hurry to start innovating together. Doing so will only lead to unnecessary ambiguity and conflicts later on.

DETERMINANTS FOR A CLEVER CONTRACT

A contract for innovation settings should be more dynamic than contracts in general, to accommodate the developments within the process. Organizations often forget to do so, which could lead to unnecessary conflicts. These in turn result in a suboptimal relationship between innovation parties.

The innovation process is constantly evolving; there is no certainty about whether you will achieve the desired result. Parties—contributors, marketeers, or distributors—may need to be added to or removed from the ecosystem in order to make things work. Will your contract accommodate this? (It should be a yes.) Does it mean that contracts should be ambiguous or open? No, but they should leave room for flexibility.

A contract does not have to be a 100-page document that is negotiated and then put inside a drawer to collect dust. We believe that a contract is not only an instrument of and for control, but especially valuable guideline in managing operations, communications, and behaviour between parties.

"WHEN THE WINDS
OF CHANGE BLOW,
SOME PEOPLE BUILD WALLS
AND OTHERS
BUILD WINDMILLS."

—Chinese proverb

SCOPING THE ACTIVITIES IN THE CONTRACT

Companies who are able to adopt and implement clever contracting—shorter, simple and visualized contracts that are used and understood by all project members, instead of their lawyers only—are able to reduce negotiation time, build more trust between parties, and shorten development times. When circumstances change during execution, there is room in the contract to adapt and manoeuvre in line with the parties' needs and wishes. It clearly describes the rights and obligations of all involved. The scope of the activities and project aims are described clearly and understandably with supporting visuals, like contractual timelines for deliveries, interfaces, and responsibilities. Future scenarios and exit options are often already discussed during negotiations. Doing this means creating clever contracts in line with your business needs.

SIMPLE, CLEAR AND FLEXIBLE CONTRACTS

More and more organizations are convinced that simple, clear and flexible contracts can be far more efficient in facilitating partnerships and collaborations for innovation. The International Association for Contract & Commercial Management (IACCM) is an organization that supports companies through awareness, advice, experience sharing, and tools to transform the way they make and manage contracts.

Tip

Bringing Design Thinking into contracts will not only simplify the matter: it will also turn the contract into a tool that non-lawyers can use in their every-day innovation management.

USE THE BUILDING BLOCKS

Apply our Building Blocks when drafting your terms and conditions, and you will see that you can easily add simplicity and flexibility to your contract while at the same time protecting each party's needs.

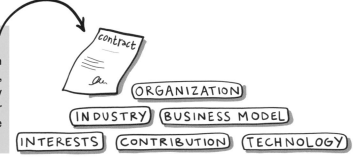

"I would only challenge the ongoing perception that contracts are 'legal'. They are not. Legal is but one stakeholder in the contracting process and contracts are business-critical, economic instruments".

— Sally Hughes

"INNOVATION CONTRACTS DETERMINE THE BEHAVIOUR OF INNOVATION TEAMS AND SET THE BOUNDARIES FOR WORKING. ISN'T THAT SOMETHING EVERYONE IN THE TEAM SHOULD KNOW? NO ONE FLIES SOLO.*"

*WITH REGARD TO THE LAST SENTENCE OF THIS QUOTE, WE WERE INSPIRED BY RICHARD MABEY FROM JURO, ONE OF THE ORGANIZATIONS ACTIVE IN LEGAL DESIGN THINKING. RICHARD MABEY'S QUOTE WAS 'LAWYERS DON'T FLY SOLO'. JURO'S WEBSITE IS WWW.JURO.COM

Tool ② LEGAL DESIGN THINKING
Start with the end user in mind

Contracts don't make innovation happen; people do. So it is essential to set them up for success. How? By designing processes and documents that support collaborating, communicating, and sense-making. This is the aim of legal design thinking. *By Stefania Passera & Helena Haapio.*

Legal design thinking is an umbrella term for merging design thinking with progressive legal thinking. It takes a proactive approach[7] to contracts and law, along with human-centred design. It focuses on supporting collaboration, driving desirable outcomes, creating opportunities, and preventing problems before they arise. This requires contracts and processes that make sense on a business level as well as to the people involved; the current contract design— or lack of which—does not meet their needs.[8]

FUNCTIONALITY AND GOOD USER EXPERIENCE FIRST

Legal design thinking stresses the importance of clarity, simplification, and visual communication to foster collaboration and innovation[9]. Visualizing helps people think, communicate, make assumptions visible, and secure understanding across disciplines. The goal is not to beautify contracts or create a false first impression of simplicity (which quickly disappears when you start reading): that amounts to putting lipstick on a pig. The goal is to create functional, readable, usable, engaging documents that users can understand and put into practice without experiencing information overload.

Definition

DESIGN THINKING

Tim Brown, CEO of IDEO, describes design thinking as 'an iterative process in which you seek to understand the user, challenge assumptions, and redefine problems in an attempt to identify alternative strategies and solutions that might not be instantly apparent with an initial level of understanding.'

Tool
② LEGAL DESIGN THINKING

BEYOND THE WALL OF CONTRACT TEXT

Contracts are not required by law to look and feel like a legal document, and do not have to be text-only. Contract visualization[10], such as adding graphs, icons, tables, charts and images to supplement text, can help navigate contract text, open up its meaning, and reinforce its message. At the contract planning stage, visualization can help identify each party's goals and expectations, align these, and capture them in a document that serves as a visible script. As long as the document clarifies the arrangement and the parties' intent to commit (for cases that have progressed past the preliminary stages), it can be presented in any way that works for the people involved.

AIM FOR ACTION

One important aspect is presenting the content in a way that makes it easy to take action. You want your teams to be fully aware of the set-up they will work in, their roles and responsibilities, and what they need to do by when. The question of how best to go about it is deeply rooted in the discipline of information design[11]. Legal information design is about organizing and displaying information in a way that maximizes its clarity and understandability. It focuses on the needs of the users, who may need to grasp both the big picture and the details—and be able to switch between these two views.

CONTRACT DESIGN PATTERNS

To transform contracts into user-friendly tools for business and to scale the results, we recommend using contract design patterns[12]. Design patterns[13] are re-usable templates of a solution to a frequent problem—something that practitioners in many fields develop, collect, and then share in pattern libraries (for example, information designers[14], interaction[15] and UX[16] designers, and software engineers).

THE MANY ADVANTAGES OF DESIGN PATTERNS

Concrete examples of robust, tested, standard ways to solve a problem; those examples can be easily copied and adapted.

Model solutions without dictating exactly how they should be implemented, allowing for flexibility and creativity.

A common language for people from different disciplines working on the same problem, so they can more readily communicate and share effective solutions with each other.

A way to spread the word about good practice that helps both experts and non-experts use, navigate, understand, and communicate their contracts more easily.

STEFANIA PASSERA & HELENA HAAPIO

Guest authors

"THE COMMERCIAL LAWYER'S GREAT UNFORCED ERROR IS THIS: BUYING INTO THE IDEA OF CONTRACTS WRITTEN BY LAWYERS, FOR LAWYERS."

—Helena Haapio & Margaret Hagan

Rob Waller[17] has written extensively on typography and page design. He and his co-authors provide examples[18] of effective layout patterns for contracts, such as left-handed headings to facilitate skimming, colour coding to signal different parts, or multi-column layered layouts for better integrating explanations, examples, and definitions. By paying attention to these things, contracts can become more engaging, useful, and usable. As for presentation, start with small steps, like a table of contents and meaningful headings and summaries.

FROM REDESIGN TO TRANSFORMATION

Legal design thinking is not only about redesigning contracts. Its human-centred methods and proactive approach can also be applied to innovating processes, services, products, and even organizations.[19] Contract design is about strategy, content and presentation, that includes structure, readability, tone of voice, typography, layout, highlights, colour coding, white space, and visualization. Your teams deserve contracts that are easy to work with. They deserve contracts that are designed, not just drafted.

RESOURCES

Visual law: what lawyers need to learn from information designers
Haapio H. & Passera S.
via blog.law.cornell.edu
direct link www.bit.ly/2QW3LGo

Design patterns for contracts: or how you've been doing contracts wrong this whole time (and how to fix it)
Haapio H. & Hagan M.
via blog.juro.com
direct link www.bit.ly/2zrzJn5

Contract Design Pattern Library
via www.legaltechdesign.com
direct link www.bit.ly/2QWKh4w

Why the time has come for design thinking and visualisation in legal documents
Passera, S. via blog.juro.com
direct link www.bit.ly/2QTeBx3

make it work!
CONTRACT DESIGN PATTERNS

These example solutions[20] can help transform contracts from dysfunctional legal documents to functional communication tools that are both useful and usable for business.

1. SWIMLANES

Swimlanes are used to show how roles, rights, tasks, responsibilities, obligations, liabilities, or remedies are distributed between different parties. They promote collaboration between parties, because they clarify who needs to do what, and whether a responsibility is shared. They provide a concise summary to help people understand their roles and responsibilities, align expectations, and monitor the contract. Parties can easily spot whether the contract is balanced and collaborative, or whether most of the responsibilities rest with just one party. An extra benefit is that swimlanes can also be used to make parties aware of areas where the contract remains silent.

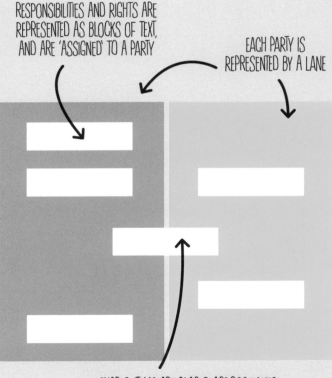

RESPONSIBILITIES AND RIGHTS ARE REPRESENTED AS BLOCKS OF TEXT, AND ARE 'ASSIGNED' TO A PARTY

EACH PARTY IS REPRESENTED BY A LANE

SHARED ITEMS ARE PLACED ACROSS LANES

THIS SECTION IS AN ABRIDGED AND MODIFIED VERSION OF HAAPIO, H. & PASSERA, S. (IN PRESS). CONTRACTS AS INTERFACES: EXPLORING VISUAL REPRESENTATION PATTERNS IN CONTRACT DESIGN. IN M. LKATZ, R.A. DOLIN & M. BOMMARITO (EDS.) LEGAL INFORMATICS. CAMBRIDGE, UK: CAMBRIDGE UNIVERSITY PRESS. IMAGES © 2019 STEFANIA PASSERA

STEFANIA PASSERA & HELENA HAAPIO

Guest authors

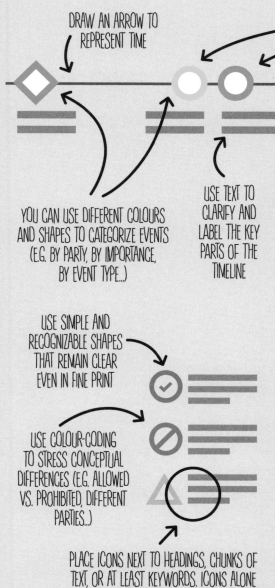

DRAW AN ARROW TO REPRESENT TIME

PLACE MARKERS FOR KEY EVENTS, IN CHRONOLOGICAL ORDER

YOU CAN USE DIFFERENT COLOURS AND SHAPES TO CATEGORIZE EVENTS (E.G. BY PARTY, BY IMPORTANCE, BY EVENT TYPE...)

USE TEXT TO CLARIFY AND LABEL THE KEY PARTS OF THE TIMELINE

USE SIMPLE AND RECOGNIZABLE SHAPES THAT REMAIN CLEAR EVEN IN FINE PRINT

USE COLOUR-CODING TO STRESS CONCEPTUAL DIFFERENCES (E.G. ALLOWED VS. PROHIBITED, DIFFERENT PARTIES...)

PLACE ICONS NEXT TO HEADINGS, CHUNKS OF TEXT, OR AT LEAST KEYWORDS. ICONS ALONE MAY NOT BE AS SELF-EVIDENT AS YOU THINK

2. TIMELINES

Timelines can be used to represent elements like a contract's duration and termination, a linear series of steps or processes taking place within a given timeframe, or a sequence of events.

Presenting events, actions, requirements, or deadlines in chronological order makes sense to readers, as it mirrors their lived experience: they can see at a glance what will happen in the future, and what course of action to take. It is also possible to use multiple, parallel timelines to gain an overview of how different, but related processes develop in time— and how they may influence each other.

3. COMPANION ICONS

Companion icons are crisp, graphic symbols that represent the meaning or function of the textual element they accompany. Icons in contracts are often highly symbolic and metaphoric, as they may refer to abstract concepts and terms. This is why we recommend using them as 'companions' to text or near headings, rather than as stand-alone icons.

Icons act as visual cues, capturing readers' attention. This way, readers can search, identify, and memorize relevant information quickly. When the same icons are used consistently throughout one or more documents, their meaning becomes familiar, so readers can identify recurrent topics and terms at a glance.

fashion forward
A CASE TO KICKSTART YOUR THINKING

Now that we have explained the opportunities legal design offers for collaboration, communication, and making sense of complexity in contracts, it is time to tie it to innovation, and particularly to IP. For the following co-creation case, we invite you to bring legal design thinking into practice. You'll find our considerations in the key; they might differ from yours and that is fine. There is no right answer.

Imagine... You are Fashion Forward, a reputable institute carrying out research and development in the field of fashion. Your institute has been testing materials, processes, and new applications for several years. It also analyzes research data to help with product development and design decision-making. Recently, your biomechanics lab has been combining this data with their own research, which tests new products and applications in different environments and provides insight into human performance. Your institute creates and owns the data analytics software, tools, and the database.

Your institute strongly encourages researchers to publish their findings in journals and present possible design decisions on conferences. If potential users are interested, they will engage your institute to perform some research for them or obtain existing findings for their industrial application. Multiple users may benefit from your research, as the findings can be applied to different applications.

PARTNERING WITH SPORTS UNLIMITED

Sports Unlimited, a company that has successfully sold sports wearables for the last sixty years, is looking to expand its range of athletic shoes to tie in with an upcoming global sports event. They have their own R&D facility and produce three new shoe designs every quarter. They hold many patents and design rights on their products. Sports Unlimited approaches your institute to collaborate on developing a new range of running shoes that will boost athletic performance. They intend to market this as a unique product during the sports season.

QUESTIONS

- What would be the leading Building Blocks in your joint-innovation analysis?
- What could a swimlane with IP rights look like?
- Can you think of icons to reinforce the understanding of commitments, rights or positions of both parties?
- What could a timeline look like?

You

INTERESTS: Research and build up IP on current fashion trends. Publish to earn reputation as a leading research institute in the fashion world. Engage users to apply findings industrially.
BUSINESS MODEL: Perform research for an industrial user, or utilise research findings for others' industrial application.

Your Partner

INTERESTS: Innovate the current product range.
TECHNOLOGY LIFE CYCLE: Develop a specific product using new technology.
BUSINESS MODEL: Boost sales of a unique product in the market.

SWIMLANE WITH IP RIGHTS	FASHION FORWARD	SPORTS UNLIMITED
BACKGROUND INFO	Free access to each other's BI for the purpose of this project only (non–transferable).	
FOREGROUND INFO	Joint ownership for IP.	
	Right to use the FI in Sports Unlimited's business model, for science and research.	Exclusive right to use the FI for commercial purposes within its own business model.
	Exclusive right to use FI outside Sport's Unlimited's business model, for any other purpose.	No use of FI in the field outside its own business model.

TIMELINE BACKGROUND INFORMATION

 PROJECT START —————— PROJECT END ——————→

Free access to each other's BI for the purpose of the project only.

Free access to each other's BI ends here (at the latest).

TIMELINE FOREGROUND INFORMATION

 PROJECT START —————— PROJECT END ——————→

You and your partner get joint ownership of generic FI created during the project.

 Multiple parties can sublicense the FI of you and your partner.

 FI created during the project within the partner's business model belongs to the partner.

FI created during the project outside of the partner's business model belongs to you.

Tool ② A deep dive into clever contracting
FOR INNOVATION AND ITS IP

In moves Think and Strategize, we identified lines of thinking ('Bringing IP into play') to help you put the model into practice while using innovation & IP strategies. Here, we would like to show how to use the business model in particular to determine and define your IP clause.

This table is an example of possible IP arrangements based on your organization's business model. For a complete overview and efficient discussions, you can prepare a similar table for your partner or partners. This IP overview is a useful tool that can be used as the basis for mandates, to equip your contracts and legal team and to speed up the process—be it for negotiating, contracting, or even the innovation itself.

Bringing IP into play

→ Generally speaking, you do not always have to own IP to use it. What organizations seem to forget sometimes is that in order to capture the value of an innovation, you need user rights and/or freedom to operate. If you own the IP, you can distribute user rights to one or many other partners in the same or different field, geography, etc. If you are a user, you gain access to IP without having to take a multitude of administrative action related to owning the IP.

→ In case of co-ownership or licensing or other distribution of IP, you could also consider adding the 'use or lose' rule. This means that a party who gets rights to use the foreground information—or any other IP in a technology or product or service—will lose the rights to do so if the IP remains unused for a certain of time (anti-shelving). You can also get creative and say that the rights will expire unless certain sales targets have been met or certain results achieved within an established time period. Such rules may even be applied in case of co-ownership, so IP ownership remains only with those co-owners who actively use it.

→ If you decide to co-own IP, you could also decide whether it is with or without accounting. In this context, 'with accounting' means that one party reports to the others what they do with the IP, for example profits made etc.

→ Two final points to decide on are whether you need the other party's consent to sublicense, and whether one party can enforce the right in legal action or whether all co-owners need to join when you sue another party. This can be arranged in the contractual agreements.

IP OPTIONS FROM YOUR PERSPECTIVE	CORE IN BUSINESS MODEL	NON-CORE IN BUSINESS MODEL
BACKGROUND INFORMATION	Grant a non–exclusive licence for the purpose of the project only.	Often not relevant or applicable.
	Grant a non–exclusive licence on favourable or commercial terms.	
FOREGROUND INFORMATION	One party owns the FI and licenses it to the other party or parties.	Sell or license out.
	Register separate same–day filings with different fields of use.	Joint ownership without accounting.
	Joint ownership with different fields of use and/or exploitation rights, with or without accounting.	
	The party who owns the BI, on which the FI is further developed, owns the FI too.	

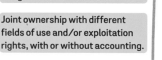

IP OPTIONS FROM BOTH PERSPECTIVES	CORE FOR BOTH PARTIES	CORE FOR ONE PARTY, NON-CORE FOR THE OTHER
BACKGROUND INFORMATION	Grant a non–exclusive licence for the purpose of the project only.	Grant a non–exclusive licence for the purpose of the project only.
	Grant a non–exclusive licence on favourable or commercial terms.	Grant a non–exclusive licence on favourable or commercial terms.
FOREGROUND INFORMATION	Separate same–day filings with different fields of use.	Claim 'core' ownership FI and license it to the other party. Possible return value for this party: other IP, percentage in profits, etc.
	Joint ownership with different fields of use and/or exploitation rights, or without accounting (in case of generic FI or shared interests).	**NON-CORE FOR BOTH PARTIES**
		Often not relevant/applicable to Background Information.
	The party who owns the BI on which the FI is further developed, owns the FI too.	Parties can sell or license Foreground Information to a third party.

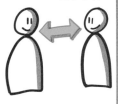

BACKGROUND INFORMATION (BI)
Knowledge/IP that is relevant to a collaborative venture or inno–vation project that is supplied by the partners at the start of the project.

FOREGROUND INFORMATION (FI)
All knowledge/IP produced within the collaborative venture or inno–vation during the project.

SIDEGROUND INFORMATION (SI)
Knowledge/IP that is relevant to a collaborative venture or inno–vation project, but produced outside the project by any of the partners during the project.

Tool ❸

ATTITUDE & ALLIANCES: CLINCH THE WIN

Innovation is a way of thinking. When innovating, you should channel your inner child: learn, explore, forgive easily, move on, and repeat! In other words, your organization must be ready to learn, explore, forgive mistakes and failures, take the lessons learnt, move on, and try again! This attitude should become part of your organizational DNA in order for your innovation strategy to be successful.

INNOVATION CULTURE

Every organization has its own innovation culture, and collaborations work better when such cultures and attitudes are respected. When Steve Jobs stepped into Pixar, he had the right attitude: 'He was flexible enough to put aside his original idea of being a computer company owner with Pixar [and to] turn it into the incredible artistic powerhouse it is.' When it comes to creating and sustaining a good innovation attitude within the teams, recognizing and retaining stronger attributes while improving upon the weaker is key.

INTERDISCIPLINARY TEAMS

Part of the innovation attitude is a greater need for strong internal and external alliances between strategists, innovators, business developers, technical and legal experts. However great an innovator is, they could not have done it alone. It is important to capitalize on the core strengths of individuals and/or departments by bringing them together. Different perspectives across disciplines add more value to the innovation process. An interdisciplinary team can provide valuable insight into the choices you have when applying our Building Blocks and Matrix to your projects. And just as importantly, such a team can instil and nurture a positive outlook on innovation in your organization.

INTERDISCIPLINARY TEAMS: MAKING THEM WORK

Multidisciplinary teams are good, but interdisciplinary teams are better: experts can learn and unlearn from each other and work together as one.

Be open Everyone must be aware of each other's strengths and weaknesses, in order to best distribute tasks between the members of the team.

Be assertive and respectful While an expert on a particular subject can assert their ideas, those of others should not be ridiculed. Such an environment allows new ideas to sprout.

Be a team A team that is strong in times of failure will work harder to succeed. The human element of the team is as important as its material goal.

"INTELLIGENT PEOPLE NEED A FOOL TO LEAD THEM. WHEN THE TEAM'S A BUNCH OF SCIENTISTS, IT'S BEST TO HAVE A PEASANT LEAD THE WAY. HIS WAY OF THINKING IS DIFFERENT. IT'S EASIER TO WIN IF YOU HAVE PEOPLE SEEING THINGS FROM DIFFERENT PERSPECTIVES."

—Jack Ma

"Simple can be harder than complex: you have to work hard to get your thinking clear to make it simple."

—Steve Jobs

ACT
summary

1. **Tool 1. Work your ecosystem:** turn on the charm! Invest in your ecosystem. The sum of all relationships determines how your organization will collaborate and innovate.

2. **Tool 2. Clever contracting:** simple & visual. Bringing Design Thinking into contracts will not only simplify the matter: it will also turn the contract in a tool that non-lawyers can use in their everyday innovation management.

3. **IP options table.** You can make different contractual IP arrangements based on your organization's business model. An overview based on each contributor's perspective and the IP they bring in will enable you to form a basis for mandates, equip your contracts and legal team, and speed up the process—be it for negotiating, contracting, or even the innovation itself.

4. **Tool 3. Attitude & alliances:** clinch the win. Your organization must be ready to learn, explore, embrace failures, take the lessons learnt, move on, and try again!

5. **Make it work.** An interdisciplinary team can provide valuable insight into the choices you face when applying our Building Blocks and Matrix to your projects. This will enable you to make the right decision in the end.

The templates on the following pages are useful in different stages of the contracting process. Alternatively, skip ahead to the next chapter to practice three case studies using our methods.

NEXT UP

CASE STUDIES

NEEDS & CONTRIBUTIONS MATRIX

This Matrix can be used in different stages: when first selecting a partner, after choosing a partner, and when finalizing the partnership. It provides valuable insights into and overviews of both parties' requirements, expectations, contributions and benefits in each stage.

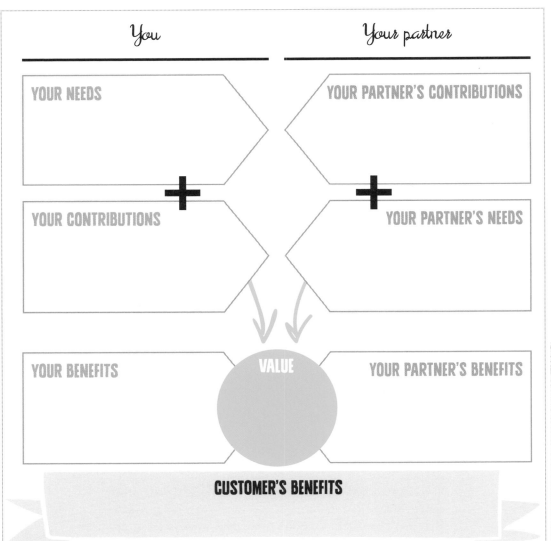

You

Your partner

YOUR NEEDS

YOUR PARTNER'S CONTRIBUTIONS

+

+

YOUR CONTRIBUTIONS

YOUR PARTNER'S NEEDS

YOUR BENEFITS

VALUE

YOUR PARTNER'S BENEFITS

CUSTOMER'S BENEFITS

COURTESY: PETER SIMOONS FROM SIMOONS & COMPANY / IVO RUTTE SIGNIFY (FORMERLY PHILIPS LIGHTING)

WEDDING CAKE MODEL BRAINSTORM TEMPLATE

This is a useful tool to identify and distribute the rights to the results of innovation between you and your partners. Wedges of IP can be distributed to several parties, so that more than one party can utilize the same product/technology/service.

Topics to analyze and decide on

	YOU	YOUR PARTNERS
REGION		
DURATION		
EXCLUSIVITY		
APPLICATION		
MARKETS		

BUILDING BLOCKS TEMPLATE

Use this template to identify and analyze the Building Blocks in your organization,
your innovation projects/cases, or even to assess your ecosystem and partners.

ORGANIZATION

YOU

YOUR PARTNERS

INDUSTRY

YOU

YOUR PARTNERS

BUSINESS MODEL

YOU

YOUR PARTNERS

INTERESTS

YOU

YOUR PARTNERS

CONTRIBUTION

YOU

YOUR PARTNERS

TECHNOLOGY

YOU

YOUR PARTNERS

IP AND INNOVATION TERM SHEET

This tool offers a quick overview on the IP resulting from your innovation. Your innovation team can
use it as a ready reference to keep track of a range of activities (contracting, sales, marketing).
Use this tool in combination with the Wedding Cake model to specifically distribute IP between parties.

	#	You	Your Partner(s)
BACKGROUND INFORMATION (BI)			
FOREGROUND INFORMATION (FI)	OPTION 1		
	OPTION 2		
	OPTION 3		
SIDEGROUND INFORMATION (SI)			

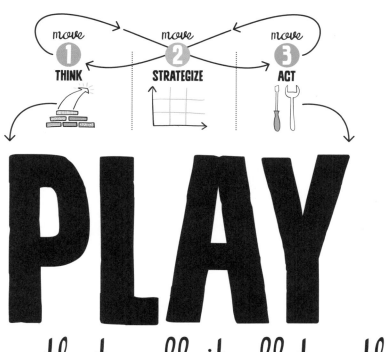

PLAY

3 cases that pull it all together

"ASKING 'WHY' CAN LEAD TO UNDERSTANDING. ASKING 'WHY NOT' CAN LEAD TO BREAKTHROUGHS."

— *Daniel Pink*

You have gotten to know our Tools, now it is time to put them to use. We have three different cases—easy, medium, and complex—to which you can apply The Three Moves. Instead of answers, we have provided you with a key to use the cases as an exercise. The key represents considerations you can take into account when designing the innovation and IP strategy, but these are not the only options. There is no one right answer, so use your creativity. Play the game by using the Building Blocks, the Matrix, and the Tools.

Case ①

PRIMECARE

PrimeCare is a popular company with a wide range of personal care products. They are far ahead of other organizations in their industry and have a strong R&D department that is one of the best in the world. PrimeCare also has a wide and strong international customer base.

The life cycle of any product they have is approximately four years, which means they must constantly improve and innovate. The innovation culture at PrimeCare is optimal; they follow several strategies. They do innovate openly sometimes, but not always.

As part of their innovation strategy, they chose to improve deodorant, an existing product in their portfolio.

QUESTION
What strategy would you choose to ignite innovation for an existing deodorant brand? To kick-start your thinking:

▢ What does your Building Block analysis look like?

▢ The innovation activity can be based on any of the boxes in the Matrix. Which would you choose and why?

▢ How could the Tools (ecosystem, contract, attitude) be used?

"TO GAIN CUSTOMER INSIGHTS, WE MUST UNDERSTAND THAT WE ARE PRISONERS OF WHAT WE KNOW AND WHAT WE BELIEVE".

—Mohanbir Sawhney

PrimeCare Building Blocks

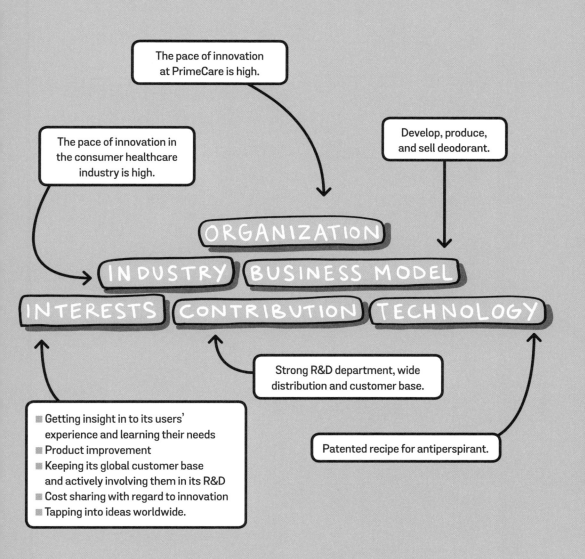

The pace of innovation at PrimeCare is high.

Develop, produce, and sell deodorant.

The pace of innovation in the consumer healthcare industry is high.

ORGANIZATION

INDUSTRY   BUSINESS MODEL

INTERESTS   CONTRIBUTION   TECHNOLOGY

Strong R&D department, wide distribution and customer base.

- Getting insight in to its users' experience and learning their needs
- Product improvement
- Keeping its global customer base and actively involving them in its R&D
- Cost sharing with regard to innovation
- Tapping into ideas worldwide.

Patented recipe for antiperspirant.

PrimeCare Matrix

	CLOSED		OPEN
REVEAL	FREE FOR PUBLIC	OPEN ACCESS RESEARCH	OPEN SOURCE
	LICENSING	COLLABORATIVE INNOVATION	CREATORS PLATFORM
GUARD	CLASSIC R & D	STEALTH INNOVATION	CROWD INNOVATION

There is no right answer. Anything could have worked (or not). This simple exercise was taken from a successful social media co-creation campaign for new deodorant, run by Nivea in 2015. They co-created with consumers to learn about stains (crowd innovation). They received feedback and identified common consumer problems through social media. This helped them identify consumer needs, and also picked ideas from the consumer base. Then they involved R&D partners to work on this feedback (collaborative innovation, or maybe even an external stealth variant) and reported back to the consumers for evaluation. As a result of all these co-creation sessions, they launched Invisible Black and White: a new deodorant that does not stain clothes and keeps skin fresh.

The interesting thing about the Nivea case is that there may not have been many give-aways in terms of IP, as the actual development was done by the internal R&D team (classical R&D). It can be speculated that even with their R&D partners, they could have engaged in selective revealing with some (a variant of collaborative innovation).

PrimeCare Tools

"KNOWING WHAT TO DO WHEN YOU DON'T KNOW WHAT TO DO."

—Jean Piaget

ECOSYSTEM

CONTRACT

ATTITUDE

This innovation case is a wonderful example of working the ecosystem, as the whole supply chain was involved in the innovation process. The customers were used as the market feedback base, whose inputs were fed to research and development partners and internal teams. The results were again taken back to the customers, thereby completing and closing the loop. This can be considered a major contributor to Nivea's success in this case.

One can assume that different contractual arrangements were made in this case. A formal and traditional contract can be expected between the R&D partners and suppliers, whereas a formal but non-traditional contract may have been used for getting feedback from customers through social media. Thus, even for a single case, multiple formats may be used depending on the other contracting party, the nature of their relationship with them, and the manner of interaction with them.

Opening up customer participation when creating a new product is a grand step that requires an open attitude within the organization too. To support this effort, they need effective feedback management, internal team response, etc. For the innovation process to run smoothly, having the right attitude is essential.

Case
❷

TAYLOR'S SMALL FAMILY BUSINESS & DAILY TROPICS

Taylor's small family business has been baking cookies and muffins for fifty years. From just three varieties of cookies ten years ago, they now sell twenty varieties of cookies and muffins, nine varieties of confectionery goods and six varieties of ready-made, fruit-based beverage mixes such as the Green Goddess smoothie mix and the Vitamin Booster mix in over 1,300 stores all over England. Almost all of their family recipes use orange peel as a special ingredient to bring out a unique flavour.

Orange peel in large quantities is processed on a daily basis to extract an essence, which is then blended in specific combinations for their recipes. The success of the business is partly owed to Taylor's invention eight years ago to process orange extract easily and quickly, to keep up with the growing demand. This year, they plan to double the number of stores where their products are available.

Daily Tropics is a large producer of fruit-based beverages in England, which belongs to a big multinational consumer food corporation. Their fruit is supplied by fifteen orchards in Spain. Orange juice is a top-selling product of Daily Tropics, and orange concentrate is a key ingredient for their juice blends. Daily Tropics is facing stiff competition from new juice producers, but has not seen a decline in sales yet. Daily Tropics wants to be prepared for this competition and ensure that they can increase current sales by at least twenty per cent in order to stay ahead of possible competitors. If they don't meet that target, the projection is that they may start facing a decline in sales within the next three years. They are considering whether new products should be added to their product portfolio, as well as looking at ancillary sources of revenue that can boost their R&D tasting department.

QUESTION

Taylor's manager has proposed working with Daily Tropics, whom he approached to discuss sourcing oranges. Daily Tropics also wants to evaluate a possible working relationship with Taylor's business.

☐ Prepare a report for Daily Tropics and/or Taylor's business to help them make a decision about working together.

☐ Evaluate what innovation options are available from the Matrix.

☐ What Tools can help implement the strategy?

"OUR INDUSTRY DOES NOT RESPECT TRADITION, IT ONLY RESPECTS INNOVATION."

—Satya Nadella

Taylor's Building Blocks

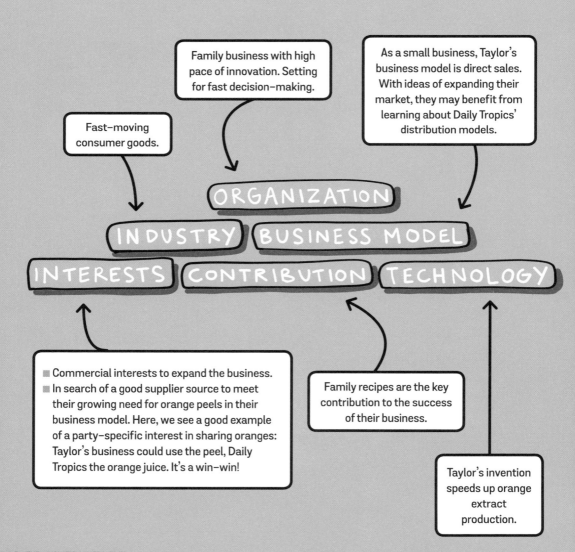

Fast-moving consumer goods.

Family business with high pace of innovation. Setting for fast decision-making.

As a small business, Taylor's business model is direct sales. With ideas of expanding their market, they may benefit from learning about Daily Tropics' distribution models.

ORGANIZATION

INDUSTRY **BUSINESS MODEL**

INTERESTS **CONTRIBUTION** **TECHNOLOGY**

- Commercial interests to expand the business.
- In search of a good supplier source to meet their growing need for orange peels in their business model. Here, we see a good example of a party-specific interest in sharing oranges: Taylor's business could use the peel, Daily Tropics the orange juice. It's a win–win!

Family recipes are the key contribution to the success of their business.

Taylor's invention speeds up orange extract production.

Daily Tropics Building Blocks

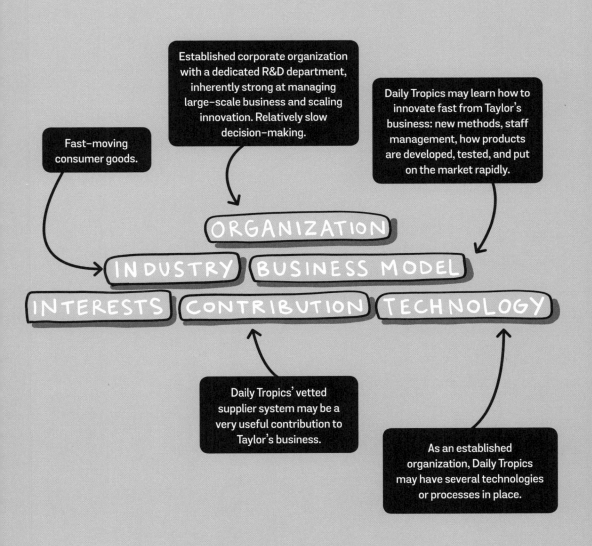

Established corporate organization with a dedicated R&D department, inherently strong at managing large-scale business and scaling innovation. Relatively slow decision-making.

Daily Tropics may learn how to innovate fast from Taylor's business: new methods, staff management, how products are developed, tested, and put on the market rapidly.

Fast-moving consumer goods.

ORGANIZATION

INDUSTRY   BUSINESS MODEL

INTERESTS   CONTRIBUTION   TECHNOLOGY

Daily Tropics' vetted supplier system may be a very useful contribution to Taylor's business.

As an established organization, Daily Tropics may have several technologies or processes in place.

Taylor's & Daily Tropics Matrix

	CLOSED		OPEN
REVEAL	FREE FOR PUBLIC	OPEN ACCESS RESEARCH	OPEN SOURCE
GUARD	LICENSING	COLLABORATIVE INNOVATION	CREATORS PLATFORM
	CLASSIC R&D	STEALTH INNOVATION	CROWD INNOVATION

Both businesses use classic R&D. Their interests are limited to what each one needs at this moment. Daily Tropics needs to increase their sales and Taylor's business wants to expand. They have some overlapping fields, which means they may engage in collaborative innovation selectively, but there are also other possibilities if they get creative. Here are some options:

1. Daily Tropics may consider picking some products from Taylor's business (like the fruit-based beverage range) to do some R&D on in order to develop their own product line, or they could give Taylor access to their distribution channels. They could choose classical R&D, collaborative innovation, selectively, open-access research, or a combination.

2. Another option for the two companies would be to enter into a licensing deal or collaborative innovation arrangement for Taylor's invention. It has been eight years since Taylor's invention; he could also benefit from additional R&D work done by Daily Tropic. Daily Tropics may gain access to some technology that might benefit their production lines.

3. They can strike a procurement deal wherein Daily Tropics can sell the peel to Taylor's business at an economical rate, so both parties benefit from reduced wastage.

4. Another option could be to strike a win–win licensing deal for procurement where Daily Tropics provides the peels for Taylor's business, if given some user rights on his invention.

Taylor's & Daily Tropics Tools

ECOSYSTEM

If both organizations are open to this collaboration, they will learn more about each other's ecosystem and may benefit in the future. For example, Daily Tropics can give Taylor's business a licence limited by duration and purpose to use its supplier system and process involved therein. Similarly, Taylor's business can help optimize Daily Tropics' processes and increase their pace of innovation, in order to compete in their industry.

CONTRACT

Any arrangements made need to be reflected in a solid, yet simple contract that adheres to quality, delivery processes, etc. The Wedding Cake model can be followed for some options, such as licensing deals or collaborative innovation arrangements for the invention, where such an arrangement is limited by geography, duration, and/or application. Both parties, being quite different in size and production scale, can have such agreements that are limited in time or broken down into phases. Exit clauses can be incorporated, so that both parties can decide at the end of each phase or limited duration if they want to continue working together. Once they are more comfortable, long-term arrangements can be made.

ATTITUDE

For Taylor's business, expanding to several stores is a big step. The family business is small in size: decisions are made quickly and innovation is rapid. They may want to see if collaborating with a big company like Daily Tropics (that is relatively slow, has to deal with bureaucracy, and innovates quite slowly) works. The attitude between two very different businesses needs to be discussed to align expectations with practice. A simple question can be so helpful: what does success look like to you? This is also why business arrangements can be made in phases, where decision moments will determine whether or not to continue collaborating.

Case

3

PLAYGO

PlayGO is a world-renowned toy manufacturer whose business consists of products that include building blocks of various types for children: bricks in fifteen shapes and fifteen colours. Their USP for about thirty years was how their play-sets triggered development, imagination, and creativity in children. The Global PlayGO community has over two million children who are part of a club receiving special offers and a magazine subscription. Additionally, its multilingual website has one million regular visitors every month.

PlayGO has been facing stiff competition from two other toy manufacturers for the last five years. A majority of their sales comes from the Americas and Europe. Last year's Christmas sales were not as expected, and the dip continues for this year's results.

THE 10 STRONGEST BRANDS

Every 2–3 years, independent market research institute Young & Rubicam conducts a comprehensive survey among families with children to identify the 10 strongest brands. The latest survey from autumn 2001 shows that PlayGO Company continues to hold 6th place.

1. Coca–Cola
2. Kellogg's
3. Disney
4. Levi's
5. Pampers
6. PlayGO
7. Fisher–Price
8. Sony
9. Nestlé
10. M&M's

PROBLEM

One of PlayGO's main issues is its lack of product diversity. To keep up with the competition, PlayGO started adding diversity to its core products by increasing the number of shapes, colours, and elements. Each shape requires a mould that costs at least $250.000, which means a lot of budget has been spent on expanding the product portfolio. In addition, heavy investments were made in the past years to develop and run two PlayGO theme parks. The returns on investment are not as high as anticipated. Each year, ten additional stores are being opened, with the hope to increase sales. Another issue was that traditional toys are being replaced by video games and online activities.

Although revenues have been increasing, net profits haven't caught up as a result. They have now reduced production capacity to match the sales activity level. Their long-term goal is to achieve stable revenue and profits with a balanced growth. To achieve this, some short-term actions are necessary.

QUESTION

You are appointed and brought in to devise actions for the business which until now engages in classic R&D, with some support from external consultants. Evaluate the list of proposed options below. Can you think of any others?
→ Build another theme park
→ Diversify and add more shapes, colours, elements
→ Work with movie and book franchises
→ Reduce the shapes, colours, elements
→ Work with users
→ Work with retailers

☐ What main Building Blocks should be considered to build a strategy for PlayGO?

☐ What innovation and IP option would you choose from the Matrix to match up or beat the competition, and why?

☐ What Tools can help implement the strategy?

PlayGO Building Blocks

- Innovative although not open
- High pace of innovation, not entirely in line with current trends
- In order to stick to PlayGO's core, i.e. building blocks, they have to increase the pace of innovation.

- They are adopting several business models to save the business
- One clearly identified model is the expansion of their product portfolio to increase sales
- Another business model is their website and membership, where they attract customers for user engagement
- Theme parks are also the result of an investment-heavy business model to increase revenues, although it is non-core.

Highly competitive toy manufacturing.

ORGANIZATION

INDUSTRY   BUSINESS MODEL

INTERESTS   CONTRIBUTION   TECHNOLOGY

PlayGO's main commercial interest is to keep up with and then beat the competition, by increasing both their revenue and their profits.

- Unique position in the toy industry in terms of building blocks
- Strong R&D department
- PlayGO has a strong customer base in two geographic regions only. Even so, the website is an important channel they could use to connect with them.

- Patented technology for building blocks and play-sets
- The life-cycle of the product seems limited, due to the availability of online activities and video games.

PlayGO Matrix

	CLOSED		**OPEN**
REVEAL	FREE FOR PUBLIC	OPEN ACCESS RESEARCH	OPEN SOURCE
LICENSING		COLLABORATIVE INNOVATION	CREATORS PLATFORM
GUARD	CLASSIC R & D	STEALTH INNOVATION	CROWD INNOVATION

Several options are provided in the case study. Here, we will evaluate three options as an example:

BUILD A THEME PARK
While this option may attract families, as well as provide an exclusive point of sales for their product and theme park merchandise, it requires heavy investment. It may take some time before seeing any Return on Investments (ROI), which means there is a risk that other competitors may move far ahead of PlayGO. Thus, a classical approach to this may not work. One possibility is that they could use these theme parks to spur more sales, instead of opening stand-alone shops. Certain limited-edition sets can be made available only at theme parks. Special events, innovation sessions with visiting customers, etc. can also generate more interest—and more revenue. Additionally, they can also use this to get instant feedback and pick ideas, as they tap into the crowd for their future innovations (crowd innovation).

WORK WITH MOVIE AND BOOK FRANCHISES
Such a collaborative innovation, where play-sets are developed based on movie or book themes, may boost sales. While it may work only for a short period of time—depending highly on the success of the movie or book in question—it could still be an interesting option to sell more expensive, limited-edition play-sets. This also means that

contractual arrangements must be put in place to ensure that the play–sets are available on time. Further, it may be important to align with two or three key franchises each year. However, the risks associated with franchises being stopped or stalled due to inherent risks in the movie and book publishing businesses require careful consideration.

WORKING WITH USERS

The biggest competition is from video games and online activities, where the users get a more intimate user experience, and may even contribute to how these games or activities are designed. Tapping into the user community for ideas, including the improvement of play–sets, helps PlayGO get direct, useful feedback from their target audience. Also, in terms of core technology, PlayGO may just revamp their products in a new interface, with a lot less investment than it would take to build a theme park.

A creators' platform may just be what PlayGO needs to give their business a boost. PlayGO can use the platform not just to connect with users, but to get ideas from them. Good ideas can be linked to an incentive, or contenders can be given some sort of recognition when their idea is used by PlayGO.

Instead of heavily investing in theme parks or expensive moulds, they could also take their products online and tie into current trends by creating games or activities. The platform could let customers build virtual sets themselves, or even let them work together on shared creations.

> ❝ I WOULDN'T HAVE SEEN IT IF I HADN'T BELIEVED IT."
>
> —*Marshall McLuhan*

PlayGO Tools

ECOSYSTEM

CONTRACT

Whether working with a movie franchise or a creators' platform, PlayGO will be tapping into a wider ecosystem. Before they step into any activity, PlayGO must ensure that they know the consequences of being part of such a network, be open to and aware of the benefits they could reap from it, as well as the security checks it requires. When working with movie and book franchises, they should take into account the risks associated with delays. Their product must be available just before the release date to create some buzz. On the other hand, there is every possibility that a movie can be shelved just before its release, putting PlayGO's production at risk. This is a different setting than standard play-set sales. The platform setting differs even more. To make the best of user engagement, their online activities must be regulated through the platform. Specific rules and guidelines must be clearly identified for each activity, in order to capitalize on PlayGO's online presence.

Collaborating with movie franchises requires several contractual arrangements to be made—especially regarding the licensed use of copyrighted images, characters, mutual use of trademarks, timely delivery, etc. Simplifying these contract elements can help manage the relationship between PlayGO and the movie franchise better than a conventional document would. For example, delivery schedules can be visualized in a timeline that lists who does what at what time, how, and to whom the input should flow; an overview of each party's rights and obligations can be listed on a single page as a summary of the contract; icons and highlighted text can be used to draw attention to a task that one of the parties must comply with, etc.

Similarly, with a creators' platform it is important to make the terms and conditions of use very explicit. Do ideas vest with the creator? Or does PlayGO capture it, because it is submitted on their platform? Can other users further develop an idea first submitted by other users? Can users communicate with each other and rank their ideas? Do users get to interact with PlayGO developers at any point, on the platform? A platform offers many possibilities, and these need to be clearly presented to its users.

PlayGO may capture the ideas that a creator submits, yet they may choose to give some sort of recognition or benefit to the creator for their contribution to PlayGO products, etc. For example, the platform could include a monthly "Hall of Fame"-styled page to bestow accolades on contributors. Recognition can also be monetary, in which the contributor receives a token amount from each sale. Such an arrangement will have to be placed on their website or other interface, to ensure that users know exactly how their ideas will be used. This is also a contract of sorts.

ATTITUDE

The move to any of the proposed activities will require a big attitude change from within PlayGO. Working with movie franchises or a creator's platform means that PlayGO must be very open to receiving and assessing ideas from others, as well as to building partnerships. Implementing them also means taking a positive approach to these ideas to enable capturing value from them.

For an organization that has worked very conservatively for many decades, sound innovation and strategy alone will not work unless the right attitude is adopted within the organization. Furthermore, it is imperative to be more agile, faster, and generally very reliable in terms of the timely delivery of the play–sets directly before, during, and after the release of a video game or movie.

THINK

STRATEGIZE

ACT

**ACKNOWLEDGEMENTS
DEEPIKA**

'Sarvam Krishnarpanam Astu'

My work on this book is not mine alone. I have had the help, support, and inspiration of many.

'Never forget a person with a pure soul; never forego the friendship of those who stood by you during distress.'

—*The Thirukkural*

Dear Mirjam,

I would not have written this book had it not been for you. Thank you for adding structure to my chaotic ideas, for sharing your wisdom and experience, and for some of the awesome moments we have shared talking about our futures!

Dear Bionda and Sara,

Thank you for being positive about our book from the first time we met! Your positivity gave us a boost of confidence! Your guidance in putting this book out into the world is much appreciated.

Dear Rachel, Femke, and Simone,

I cannot thank you enough for bringing our words to life. At each stage of our review, I've reveled in the work you have done. You have made working on this book a greatly enjoyable experience.

Dearest Sumi and Jeyho,

Thank you for EVERYTHING you have done for me! I am forever indebted to you for your love.

My dear thatha, N.K.Kondalswamy,

Thank you for always dreaming big for me. I hope I have made you proud!

Dear family in Madras,

Your love, care, and timely help through the years will never be forgotten.

Dear Sivaraman Uncle,

Thank you for always wishing the best for me! I'm forever grateful for the years of love and kindness.

Dear Gautam,

As much as you annoy me, I have enjoyed our time together in a strange new country for the last four years. It has been the best for us as siblings! Thank you for your patience, understanding, and care, even when I get crazy.

Dear Aswin, Prem, and Fathima,

Thank you for being the constants in my life! I may never tell you so, but thanks for being my pillars of support.

Dear Nisha,

You may never read this book, but I know you'll probably have the most copies of it. I am truly blessed to have your unconditional love! Thank you, Dodo!

Dear Jinny,

From our time at Middelstegracht to now, thank you for being my friend and family in the Netherlands!

Dear Karin aka work mom,

Thank you for your endless love and care. You're my rock!

Dear Anish,

Someday soon you will be old enough to read this book. I hope you will be as excited about it then as you are now!

Dear Mrs. Mary Chapman,

from Campbelltown Performing Arts High School, NSW, Australia, (1999–2000)

I do not know where you are now, but thank you for believing in me. Your prophecy that I will someday write something others will read has come true.

Dear friends, teachers, and colleagues,

Thank you for your enthusiasm, inspiration, and support!

Dear Mannamma and Anand,

Thank you for the many years of service!

Dear day dreamers, strong voices that speak for the voiceless, and altruists,

The world needs more people like you. Thank you for everything you do. My respects!

ACKNOWLEDGEMENTS
MIRJAM

What a great journey it was to write this book! The support of many people made it possible to get it done and published. It felt like standing on the shoulders of giants.

Dear Deepika,
This book would never have been written without your continuous help, energy sparks, and superb writing and research skills! Thank you for spending so much time and effort on this journey and for believing in the business value of my simple, common sense ideas about innovation and IP. I feel very lucky and grateful to be your co-author.

Dear co-workers,
I would like to thank all of the wonderful colleagues, great managers, inspiring team members, customers, suppliers and partners I had the luck to work with over the last twenty years. You taught me that you never fly solo and that there is no I in TEAM.

Dear Rachel and Femke,
In creating this book, two very special and gifted ladies helped us to make it look, read and feel the way we dreamed it to be. You exceeded our expectations with your art direction, design, and editing; what a great team you are!

Dear Simone,
Thank you for co-creating the visuals that tell our story in such a playful way. Your creative inputs have been very valuable.

Dear Ashley,
Thank you for doing a great job copy-editing our book!

Dear Bionda and Sara,
We are thankful that you believed our message should be spread around the world. And what great books you publish! We are proud to be BIS authors now, and strongly feel you understand and engage in elegantly enabling your ecosystem.

Dear reviewers,
We would like to thank all the great people who took the time to review our book and who inspired us to further improve it. Your positive and critical feedback made us—and, hopefully, our book—stronger. All our thanks!

Dear Helena and Stefania,
What a gesture that you were willing to introduce us in the world of Legal Design. We gladly applied your bright ideas about legal design thinking and design patterns to innovation and IP. Quite new for the legal world! We hope you will inspire our readers as much as you have inspired us.

Dear Peter and Ivo,

Thank you for letting us borrow your Needs & Contributions Matrix; we are so happy to offer the reader your powerful tool.

Dear Mr. Jeremy de Beer,

Your 2014 webinar on YouTube inspired us to create our Innovation Matrix. Thank you for giving us the opportunity to stand on your shoulders.

Dear Ellen, Cristhel, mum and dad,

Thank you for being my family, for your supportive and inspiring energy to pick up new and creative things. You are my roots and my basis for reflection, for feeling at home and having fun together.

Dear Henrike,

From the age of twelve, you helped me find out who I am, what I want and what I love to do by always being positive, enthusiastic, and critical when needed. Thank you for being who you are, wherever you are!

Dear friends,

Thank you for being a part of my journey, adding joy and happiness throughout the years!

Dear Harris and Sijds,

I remember the days when I was finishing my thesis, when you were only a toddler and a baby. Now you are eleven and fourteen, and it is so nice to see your interest and support regarding my 'hobby'. I would like to repeat what I wrote to you in 2007: I hope you too will find something in life that you love to do; something that matters to you and that makes you happy. It will make you feel rich every day, since loving your work is good business. I hope I'll always be there for you to lend my shoulders to stand on; to support you in living your dreams and becoming who you are.

Dear Menno,

Thank you for supporting me in this journey of writing a book, in addition to being my partner in life and a great father to our sons. Thank you for being there for me always. Love you!

FOOTNOTES & REFERENCES

INTRODUCTION

1. Takenaka, T. (2013). *Intellectual property in common law and civil law.* Cheltenham: Edward Elgar Pub. Ltd., p.419.

2. Thrivable.net. (2010). *Network Thinking: Interview with Valdis Krebs | Thrivable.* [online] Available at: http://thrivable.net/2010/11/network-thinking-interview-with-valdis-krebs/ [Accessed 17 Oct. 2018].

3. Chesbrough, H. (2003). *Open innovation: the new imperative for creating and profiting, from technology:* Harvard Business School Press, Boston.

4. Chesbrough, H. (2006). *Open business models.* Boston: Harvard Business School Press, pp.108-111.

5. George, B. (2017). *VUCA 2.0: A Strategy For Steady Leadership In An Unsteady World.* [online] Forbes. Available at: https://www.forbes.com/sites/hbsworkingknowledge/2017/02/17/vuca-2-0-a-strategy-for-steady-leadership-in-an-unsteady-world/#68ea888913d8 [Accessed 17 Oct. 2018].

6. M. Kalanje, C. (n.d.). *Role of Intellectual Property in Innovation and New Product Development.* [online] WIPO. Available at: http://www.wipo.int/sme/en/documents/ip_innovation_development_fulltext.html [Accessed 17 Oct. 2018].

MOVE 1: THINK

1. De Beer, J. (2014). *Intellectual Property Strategies for Open Innovation.* [online] Curvetube. Available at: http://curvetube.com/Jeremy_De_Beer_Intellectual_Prop-%20erty_Strategies_for_Open_Innovation/RlgIGLmV5Pw.video [Accessed 17 Oct. 2018].

2. Patton, B., Ury, W. and Fisher, R. (2014). *Getting to yes.* New York: Penguin Books.

3. Phys.org. (2004). *Nokia and Vodafone Team Up on Mobile Java Standards.* [online] Available at: https://phys.org/news/2004-08-nokia-vodafone-team-mobile-java.html [Accessed 17 Oct. 2018].

4. Zhang, J. and Golbeck, J. (2016). *The Facebook–PayPal Partnership: Who Benefits Most? - Knowledge@Wharton.* [online] Wharton. Available at: http://knowledge.wharton.upenn.edu/article/the-facebook-paypal-partnership-who-benefits-most/ [Accessed 17 Oct. 2018].

5. https://www.holstcentre.com/about-holst-centre/holst-centre-in-a-nutshell/

6. http://www.thesgc.org [Accessed 17 Oct. 2018].

7. Castle-Clarke, S. (2014). *A new model for open innovation: the Structural Genomics Consortium - EuroScientist journal.* [online] EuroScientist. Available at: https://www.euroscientist.com/a-new-model-for-open-innovation-the-structural-genomics-consortium/ [Accessed 17 Oct. 2018].

8. Surreynanosystems.com. (n.d.). *FAQs | Surrey NanoSystems.* [online] Available at: https://www.surreynanosystems.com/vantablack/faqs [Accessed 17 Oct. 2018].

9. Supra, note 4 (INTRODUCTION). Chesbrough, H. (2006). *Open business models.* Boston: Harvard Business School Press, pp.108-111.

10. Alexy, O., Criscuolo, P. and Salter, A. (2009). *Does IP Strategy Have to Cripple Open Innovation?* [online] MIT Sloan Management Review. Available at: https://sloanreview.mit.edu/article/does-ip-strategy-have-to-cripple-open-innovation/ [Accessed 17 Oct. 2018].

11. Laursen, K. and Salter, A. (2014). The paradox of openness: Appropriability, external search and collaboration. *Research Policy*, 43(5), pp.867-878.

12. Sushil., Connell, J. and Burgess, J. (2016). *Flexible Work Organizations.* New Delhi: Springer India, p.256.

MOVE 2: STRATEGIZE

1. Spruijt, J. (2011). *What Steve Jobs did (not do) for Open Innovation.* [online] Open Innovation – Keynotes, Masterclasses & Games. Available at: http://www.openinnovation.eu/06-12-2011/what-steve-jobs-did-not-do-for-open-innovation/ [Accessed 17 Oct. 2018].

2. Supra, note 1 (THINK). De Beer, J. (2014). *Intellectual Property Strategies for Open Innovation.* [online] Curvetube. Available at: http://curvetube.com/Jeremy_De_Beer_Intellectual_Prop-%20erty_Strategies_for_Open_Innovation/RlglGLm-V5Pw.video [Accessed 17 Oct. 2018].

3. CNET. (2005). *IBM looks for profit in free patents.* [online] Available at: https://www.cnet.com/news/ibm-looks-for-profit-in-free-patents/ [Accessed 17 Oct. 2018].

4. Chambers, C. (2014). *Tesla Giving Away Its Patents Makes Sense.* [online] Forbes. Available at: https://www.forbes.com/sites/investor/2014/06/13/tesla-giving-away-its-patents-makes-sense/ [Accessed 17 Oct. 2018].

5. Ibid.

6. Asay, M. (2013). *Is Facebook The World's Largest Open Source Company?* [online] ReadWrite. Available at: https://readwrite.com/2013/10/17/is-facebook-the-worlds-largest-open-source-company/ [Accessed 17 Oct. 2018].

7. Morikawa, M. (2016). *16 Examples of Open Innovation – What Can We Learn From Them?* [online] Viima.com. Available at: https://www.viima.com/blog/16-examples-of-open-in-novation-what-can-we-learn-from-them [Accessed 17 Oct. 2018].

8. Asay, M. (2015). *Is Facebook The World's Largest Open Source Company? - ReadWrite.* [online] ReadWrite. Available at: https://readwrite.com/2015/10/17/is-facebook-the-worlds-largest-open-source-company/ [Accessed 17 Oct. 2018].

9. Ideaconnection.com. (2011). *Lego Success Built on Open Innovation - Open Innovation success stories.* [online] Available at: https://www.ideaconnection.com/open-innova-tion-success/Lego-Success-Built-on-Open-Innova-tion-00258.html [Accessed 17 Oct. 2018].

10. Ibid.

11. Supra, note 8 (THINK). Chesbrough, H. (2006). *Open business models.* Boston: Harvard Business School Press, pp.108-111.

12. Wagner, S. (2015). *Are 'Patent Thickets' Smothering Innovation?.* [online] Yale Insights. Available at: https://insights.som.yale.edu/insights/are-patent-thickets-smothering-in-novation [Accessed 17 Oct. 2018].

13. The term 'Wedding Cake Model' was introduced at the workshop "From idea to market" given by Wouter Pijzel from NOVU, the Dutch organization for inventors.

14. Martinez, M., Lazzarotti, V., Manzini, R. and García, M. (2014). *Open innovation strategies in the food and drink industry: determinants and impact on innovation performance.* International Journal of Technology Management, 66(2/3), p.212.

15. Brant, J. and Lohse, S. (2014). *The Open Innovation Model ICC Innovation and Intellectual Property Research Paper No. 2.* [online] Cdn.iccwbo.org. Available at: https://cdn.iccwbo.org/content/uploads/sites/3/2014/10/THE-OPEN-INNOVA-TION-MODEL-1.pdf [Accessed 17 Oct. 2018].

16. Henkel, J. (2006). *Selective revealing in open innovation processes: The case of embedded Linux.* Research Policy, 35(7), pp.953-969.

17. Supra, note 7 (STRATEGIZE). Morikawa, M. (2016). *16 Examples of Open Innovation – What Can We Learn From Them?* [online] Viima.com. Available at: https://www.viima.com/blog/16-examples-of-open-innovation-what-can-we-learn-from-them [Accessed 17 Oct. 2018].

MOVE 3: ACT

1. Adner, R. (2012) *The Wide Lens: A New Strategy for Innovation*, Penguin group, UK.

2. Allen, F. (2012). *Why Great Innovations Fail: It's All in the Ecosystem*. [online] Forbes. Available at: https://www.forbes.com/sites/frederickallen/2012/03/05/why-great-innovations-fail-its-their-ecosystem/#4867a9107f3c [Accessed 17 Oct. 2018].

3. Jackson, D. (2011). *What is an Innovation Ecosystem?* [online] Erc-assoc.org. Available at: http://erc-assoc.org/sites/default/files/topics/policy_studies/DJackson_Innovation%20Ecosystem_03-15-11.pdf [Accessed 17 Oct. 2018].

4. Hope.haier.com. (n.d.). *HOPE 开放创新平台*. [online] Available at: http://hope.haier.com/ [Accessed 17 Oct. 2018].

5. Nunes, P. and Downes, L. (2016). *At Haier and Lenovo, Chinese-Style Open Innovation*. [online] Forbes. Available at: https://www.forbes.com/sites/bigbangdisruption/2016/09/26/at-haier-and-lenovo-chinese-style-open-innovation/ [Accessed 17 Oct. 2018].

6. Ibid.

7. Siedel, G. and Haapio, H. (2016). *Proactive law for managers*. Abingdon, Oxon: Routledge.

8. Siedel, G. and Haapio, H. (2011). *Proactive Law for Managers: A Hidden Source of Competitive Advantage*. 1st ed. Routledge.

9. Ducato, R, Haapio, H, Hagan, M, Palmirani, M, Passera, S, Rossi, A (2018). *The Legal Design Manifesto*, [online] Available at: https://www. legaldesignalliance.org/ [Accessed 17 Oct. 2018].

10. Passera, S. (2017). Beyond the wall of contract text – Visualizing contracts to foster understanding and collaboration within and across organizations. Aalto University School of Science. [online] Available at: http://urn.fi/URN:IS-BN:978-952-60-7528-0 [Accessed 17 Oct. 2018].

11. Information Design Association (n.d.) Definitions. [online] Infodesign. Available at: http://www.infodesign.org.uk/What-is-information-design/definitions [Accessed 17 Oct. 2018].

12. Haapio, H & Hagan, M (2016) *Design patterns for Contracts*. In Schweighofer, E. et al. (eds), Networks. Proceedings of the 19th International Legal Informatics Symposium IRIS 2016. pp. 381–388. Österreichische Computer Gesellschaft OCG:Wien.

13. Alexander, C, Ishikawa, S, Silverstein, M, Jacobson, M, Fiksdahl-King, I, & Angel, S (1977). *A Pattern language – towns, buildings, construction*. New York: Oxford University Press.

14. Waller, R & Delin, J (2011). *A pattern language for describing documents*, Technical paper 4, Simplification Center, April 2011, [online] Available at: https://www.reading.ac.uk/web/FILES/simplification/tech_paper_4.pdf [Accessed 17 Oct. 2018].

15. Pan, Y, & Stolterman, E (2013). *Pattern language and HCI: expectations and experiences, in CHI 2013 extended abstracts on human factors in computing systems*, pp.1989–1998, New York: Association of Computing Machinery (ACM).

16. Malone, E (2017). *A history of patterns in user experience design. Filling in some missing pieces*, Tangible UX [online] Medium. Available at: https:/medium.com/tangible-ux/a-history-of-patterns-in-user-experience-design-f21f7eaabb83 [Accessed 17 Oct. 2018].

17. Waller, R (n.d.) Writing. [online] Available at: http:/www.robwaller.org/writing.html [Accessed 17 Oct. 2018].

18. Waller, R, Waller, J, Haapio, H, Crag, G, & Morrisseau, S (2016) *Cooperation through clarity: designing simplified contracts*. Journal of Strategic Contracting and Negotiation, Vol. 2, Issue 1–2 (Special Issue: Contracting for Innovation and Innovating Contracts), pp. 48–68.

19. Hagan, M (n.d.). *Types of design. law by design*. [online] Lawbydesign. Available at: http://www.lawbydesign.co/en/legal-design/#types [Accessed 17 Oct. 2018].

20. This section is an abridged and modified version of Haapio, H. & Passera, S. (in press). *Contracts as interfaces: exploring visual representation patterns in contract design* in M. J. Katz, R.A. Dolin & M. Bommarito (Eds.) *Legal Informatics*, Cambridge, UK: Cambridge University Press.

GUEST AUTHORS: LEGAL DESIGN THINKING
PAGES 93–97

STEFANIA PASSERA is an information designer specialized in contract visualization, contract design, and legal design. Her firm, Passera Design, helps clients worldwide create user–friendly, engaging contracts and legal documents. She is the initiator of Legal Design Jam (www.legaldesignjam.com), and a Visiting Researcher at the Helsinki University Legal Tech Lab.

HELENA HAAPIO is a contract innovator and a Proactive Law pioneer. She is Associate Professor of Business Law, University of Vaasa, and director of Lexpert Ltd (www.lexpert.com). Her research and practice focus on enhancing the functionality, usability, and UX of contracts.

Together, they are on a mission to transform contracts from legal instruments to valuable business tools. They are both among the original signatories of the Legal Design Manifesto (www.legaldesignalliance.org)